British History in Per:
General Editor: Jerem

Titles continued overleaf

List continued from previous page

Richard Rex *Henry VIII and the English Reformation*
G. R. Searle *The Liberal Party: Triumph and Disintegration,1886–1929*
Paul Seaward *The Restoration, 1660–1668*
John Stuart Shaw *The Political History of Eighteenth-Century Scotland*
W. M. Spellman *John Locke*
William Stafford *John Stuart Mill*
Robert Stewart *Party and Politics, 1830–1852*
Bruce Webster *Medieval Scotland*
Ann Williams *Kingship and Government in Pre-Conquest England*
John W. Young *Britain and European Unity, 1945–92*
Michael B. Young *Charles I*

Please note that a sister series, *Social History in Perspective*, is now available.
It covers the key topics in social, cultural and religious history.

ISBN 0-333-56763-3
ISBN 978-0-3335-6763-0
Transferred to Digital Printing 2007

You can receive future titles in this series as they are published by placing a
standing order. Please contact your bookseller or, in case of difficulty, write to us
at the address below with your name and address, the title of the series and one or
both of the ISBNs quoted above.

Customer Services Department, Macmillan Distribution Ltd
Houndmills, Basingstoke, Hampshire RG21 6XS, England

THE GLORIOUS REVOLUTION

EVELINE CRUICKSHANKS

First published in Great Britain 2000 by
MACMILLAN PRESS LTD
Houndmills, Basingstoke, Hampshire RG21 6XS and London
Companies and representatives throughout the world

A catalogue record for this book is available from the British Library.

ISBN 0–333–56762–5 hardcover
ISBN 0–333–56763–3 paperback

First published in the United States of America 2000 by
ST. MARTIN'S PRESS, INC.,
Scholarly and Reference Division,
175 Fifth Avenue, New York, N.Y. 10010

ISBN 0–312–23008–7 clothbound
ISBN 0–312–23009–5 paperback

Library of Congress Cataloging-in-Publication Data
Cruickshanks, Eveline.
The glorious revolution / Eveline Cruickshanks.
p.   cm. — (British history in perspective)
Includes bibliographical references (p.) and index.
ISBN 0–312–23008–7 (cloth) — ISBN 0–312–23009–5 (pbk.)
1. Great Britain—History—Revolution of 1688. I. Title. II. Series.

DA452.C87   2000
941.06'7—dc21

99–048546

This book is printed on paper suitable for recycling and made from fully managed and
sustained forest sources.

10   9   8   7   6   5   4   3   2   1
09 08 07 06 05 04 03 02 01 00

Printed in Hong Kong

CONTENTS

INTRODUCTION

The Whig interpretation of the Glorious Revolution, enshrined as part of the unwritten constitution by T. B. Macaulay in his *History of England from the Accession of James II* in the mid-nineteenth century (standard edition by C. H. Firth, 6 vols, 1913–15) and his great nephew G. M. Trevelyan, in his *The English Revolution, 1688–89* (1938), laid down that it was responsible for political liberty, constitutional stability, economic progress and religious freedom. For Macaulay, James II was the villain and William of Orange was the hero. Macaulay was not original in this view – he adopted uncritically the interpretation of Whig ideology current in the eighteenth century. It was this which led Charles James Fox, the most eminent parliamentarian in opposition to George III's government, to see the French Revolution of 1789 as a re-enactment of the Glorious Revolution. Others took a different view. Dr Johnson, the celebrated eighteenth-century Tory thinker and writer, deplored the fact that the English, in order to maintain their religion in 1688, had to submit to 'one of the most worthless scoundrels that ever existed' and one who was 'not the lawful sovereign'.[1] Tom Paine, an ardent supporter of the American and French Revolutions and the author of *The Rights of Man*, for his part, and other radicals, thought William III's invasion had enslaved the people no less than William the Conqueror's in 1066. Similarly, Richard Carlisle, a Deist (one who believed in the existence of God but rejected Revelation), wrote at the end of the eighteenth century that the Glorious Revolution began the rot, that William III was an usurper, and that James II was the rightful king.[2] Christopher Hill, a Marxist historian, has seen it as a mere palace revolution or a *coup d'état*. Tony Benn at one end of the political spectrum and Jonathan Clark at the other (in a debate on BBC Radio 4 held on 20 July 1988), came to much the same conclusion. Historians of the Civil Wars have assumed that the religious and political conflicts they studied closely in the earlier years of the seventeenth century were

1

somehow solved after 1689 and that, as in novels, they all lived happily
ever after. An American historian, Alice Pinkham, in *William III and the
Respectable Revolution* (1954), first questioned Macaulay's interpretation
and was much derided as a result. It was not until the 1970s that Macaulay and Trevelyan were more widely challenged. Diplomatic historians
began to see the Revolution as part of a vast diplomatic campaign on the
part of William of Orange to secure the power of the British army and
navy in the Dutch struggle against Louis XIV, the more urgent in view of
France having reached naval parity with the Dutch.

Was the Revolution a selfless act on the part of the Prince of Orange to
restore British liberties after the encroachments of an absolutist James?
Was it a Dutch conquest? Was it achieved by what might be termed the
most successful confidence trick in British history? One thing is certain:
William of Orange did not come over to England by popular demand.
The thick smokescreen which became the Whig interpretation was put
up very quickly to mask what had really happened. Yet doubts remained,
so that Blair Worden could write: 'the deposition of James II left the English with a guilty conscience, which they have never shaken off'.[3]

The Tercentenary of the Glorious Revolution in 1988 was celebrated
wholeheartedly in America and the Netherlands, but mutedly in Britain,
mainly because of the Irish troubles which arose out of it. Anglo-Dutch
friendship was praised, with special emphasis on the introduction into
England of 'Dutch-style' gardens, which bore more than a passing
resemblance to Louis XIV's gardens at Versailles. Even the famous
gardens at Levens in Westmorland, laid out for James Grahme, James II's
Privy Purse, in 1685, are being described as Dutch-style gardens. The
politicians differed on what the Revolution had meant. The Lord Chancellor, Lord Hailsham, hailed it as the foundation of our 'system of parliamentary democracy under a constitutional monarch', while Lord
Grimond, for the Liberals, called it 'a *coup d'état* carried out largely by
appealing to religious bigotry, and treachery'.[4] The Tercentenary Celebrations or commemorations, however, have re-examined or discovered
new aspects of what took place. The most spectacular revelations were
made by Jonathan Israel, who thought it had been one of the most
inglorious of revolutions.

One of the most difficult tasks is to separate the short-term effects of
the Revolution – the administrative chaos and financial corruption of
William's reign – from the long-term effects of bringing about the financial revolution and the emergence of Britain as a world power. It is a tall
order for any historian, but I will attempt to address these questions, at

the risk of achieving only partial success. Several of the books produced to mark the Tercentenary anniversary have ignored Scotland and Ireland, where the impact of the Revolution was greatest. I have attempted to give a short account of the effects of the Revolution on both kingdoms. The European context, so long neglected by insular British historians, which was brought out by John Carswell in *The Descent on England* (1969), has been taken much further by Jonathan Israel and Dale Hoak. What was ignored by others and which I have added is the mass emigration of British Jacobites to the continent of Europe after 1689, first to France, and then to Spain, Russia, Prussia and Sweden. This exile greatly exceeded that of the Huguenots (the French Protestants) in point of numbers, and the contribution they made to the life of the host countries surpassed that of the Huguenots in England. At a time when Britain is increasingly involved in the European Union, the Jacobite exiles – soldiers, seamen, merchants and bankers – were, it seems to me, the first real Europeans.

1

THE RESTORATION: RELIGIOUS AND POLITICAL CONFLICTS IN THE REIGN OF CHARLES II

The Restoration of 1660 was greeted with almost universal joy after the chaos of the Civil Wars and the failed constitutional experiments of the Interregnum, as heralding the return to order and legitimacy. The Acts and Ordinances of the Interregnum had banned all forms of pleasure, however innocent, and most types of folk culture. Christmas was restored, together with the other traditional feasts. Charles II was a realist and he accepted that many of the changes made since 1640 were irreversible, especially the sale of forfeited royalist estates, many of which had changed hands several times. Only crown and church lands had to be given back. Nor did he make the mistake of employing only Royalists and excluding a substantial part of the political nation, as George I and George II were to do by employing only Whigs after 1715. To some extent, he compensated royalist sufferers with pensions and Household places. Experienced men in the administration, the navy and the army were continued in office even if they had been Parliamentarians. Charles II's power was more apparent than real, with a tiny army and a small navy, understandably, since army rule had became anathema. The downside was that this prevented Britain from achieving the status of a first-class power. Even the ultra-loyalist Cavalier Parliament had not voted him a revenue sufficient to adequately cover state expenditure.[1] Besides, Lord Chancellor Clarendon's and Lord Treasurer Southampton's practice of giving offices for life often prevented effective parliamentary management. Charles did carry out some reforms to cut the cost of his Household. This was urgent, as he had to give up Purveyance, whereby members of the Household could get victuals below the market rate. After the deprivations of exile, however, Charles was unwilling to give up his personal pleasures. The Dissenters and the more religious people in the Church of England were shocked at the string of mistresses he flaunted so publicly, but many more joined in the general laxity after so much restraint. Nor was he willing or probably able to confront vested interests.

Charles was constrained in England not only by Parliament, but by the customary rights and privileges which limited the French as well as the English *anciens régimes*. The Ancient Constitution, embodying common law, custom, and judicial rulings, was regarded as the guardian of rights and liberties. There is little evidence that Charles sought to overturn the foundation of the Church and constitution to establish Catholicism or absolutism. In any case, Charles II, or Louis XIV come to that, could not become absolute in the way the Tsars of Russia, the Kings of Prussia or the Sultans of Turkey were absolute rulers.

The great unsolved problem after 1660 was religion. The Church of England, outlawed and persecuted during the political and religious upheavals, was the Church to which the vast majority of people in England and Wales belonged. It was restored as the national Church and it preached divine hereditary right and non-resistance and the cult of Charles I as Charles the Martyr. It enjoyed a monopoly of office in Church and State. The minority of sects, such as Independents, Baptists and Quakers, remained hostile to the regime or plotted actively against it. The Presbyterians, on the other hand, had worked and plotted for a Restoration, but they could not obtain comprehension within the Church of England. In this situation, using the word 'Protestant' on its own begs more questions than it solves. Until Bishop Compton's census of 1676, the government and contemporaries generally greatly overestimated the numbers of Protestant Dissenters.[2] The Roman Catholic minority, whose exact number is impossible to calculate as persecution made it prudent for them to lie low, had been the most active and loyal of the Royalists. It has been suggested that one-seventh of the English gentry and aristocracy were Roman Catholics.[3] Anti-popery, fed by the paranoia of owners of monastic lands, who feared any Catholic king would force them to give them back, the popularity of Foxe's *Book of Martyrs*, and denunciations of the Church of Rome as the 'Whore of Babylon' and a threat to Britain's independence, cast Roman Catholics in the role of perpetual traitors and scapegoats. The terms of the Secret Treaty of Dover of 1670, by which

Charles was to declare himself a Catholic at a time convenient to himself in exchange for a subsidy from Louis XIV of France, were not disclosed. Charles II was forced to abandon the Declaration of Indulgence of 1672, which would have given freedom to worship in private for Catholics and in public for Protestant Dissenters. It led to the passing of the Test Act of 1673, which forced the resignation as Lord High Admiral of Charles's brother and heir, James Duke of York, a Catholic convert since 1669 who was regarded as the founder of the Royal Navy. Protestant Dissenters fared better, as in the absence of commissioners, the Corporation Act went largely unenforced after 1663 and lapsed in 1667, so that many corporate boroughs remained in nonconformist hands. The Conventicle Acts, on the other hand, were enforced and caused hardship to Protestant Dissenters.

After the disasters of the Third Anglo-Dutch War (1672–74), undertaken at a time when the Dutch were regarded by many as the enemy of Britain and the chief threat to its commerce, Charles II and his ministers followed a policy of peace. The advent of Sir Thomas Osborne, lst Earl of Danby, as Lord Treasurer in the years 1673–79, saw the dawn of a new era, with more efficient Parliamentary management. He sought to produce a stable majority for the Court in Parliament through a policy of friendship with France, Charles II's favoured option, and Anglican ascendancy, with some concessions to Roman Catholics and Dissenters, though he himself supported the renewal of the Conventicle Act. His ministry was based on sound churchmanship, sound finance and the Protestant interest. To secure a reliable majority in the Commons, he adopted tactics which foreshadowed those of Robert Harley, Queen Anne's First Minister, or of Sir Robert Walpole, Prime Minister to George I and George II. He organised the counting of heads in the Commons, the systematic use of royal patronage (though hampered by the grant life patents), and whipping, which had hitherto been practised only haphazardly. Disregarding the Earl of Essex's advice that in English elections 'recommendations from the Court rather hinder than help one to be chosen', he intervened actively in elections to secure the return of reliable Members and appreciated the importance of the elections committee as a way of unseating opponents. Nowhere were Danby's friends so active as in that committee. The improvement of the royal finances enabled pensions and salaries to be paid regularly for the first time in the reign, with significant results on the management of Parliament.[4] The King thought his nephew, the Prince of Orange, too Dutch and too much of a Calvinist for his liking, and deeply resented his dealings with 'malcontents' in

England.[5] Yet Danby successfully defused the activities of William of Orange and his friends among the First Whigs by negotiating the marriage of Mary, daughter of James, Duke of York, with the Prince of Orange, which was popular and helped to secure the largest Parliamentary grant of the reign. At the time, it was less popular with Mary, who wept for a day and a half at the prospect of marriage to the hunchbacked, hook-nosed prince with an asthmatic cough. Danby was hampered, however, by the ambiguous nature of the King's foreign policy by having to agree to seeking subsidies from Louis XIV (though Charles was being paid for what he wanted to do anyway) and the unpopular policies of Lauderdale in Scotland. The Speaker, Sir Edward Seymour, his personal enemy, was often able to check his measures. In the Lords, with the help of the bishops, new creations of peerages and the King's personal interventions, he was not challenged. In 1677, as Louis's armies progressed through the Spanish Netherlands (modern Belgium), fears for the safety of the Dutch Republic were renewed. Against all expectations Charles began to prepare for war, though he feared the Commons would engage him in war and then deny him the money to fight it, the perennial dilemma of Stuart kings. Charles was expected to defeat Louis XIV with less than 8000 troops, whereas William III could not do so with over 90 000. Louis XIV, fearing above all that the King and Parliament might unite against France, began, through his ambassador, Barrillon, to buy out leading opponents of the Court to prevent a war against France, whilst ostensibly clamouring for it in Parliament. Among those who took French bribes were William, Lord Russell, William, Lord Cavendish, Algernon Sidney, William Sacheverell, Sir Edward Harley and others.[6] The deviousness of seventeenth-century politicians never ceases to amaze. When Sir John Dalrymple published their names and the sums they received from Louis from the original documents in the French Ministry of Foreign Affairs it was this, rather than the Whig junto's (ministers, from the Spanish *junta*) intrigues with James II in exile, which most shocked eighteenth-century Whigs. They could not believe that, in the words of John Wilkes: 'Lord Russell intrigued with the Court of Versailles and Algernon Sidney took money from it.'[7] During the recess, Charles signed a treaty with Louis to prorogue Parliament and disband recently raised forces. Louis complained of the marriage with William of Orange and the alliance with the Dutch, but the threat of war did help to make Louis settle for peace and for less territory than he had hoped for.[8]

2

THE POPISH PLOT AND THE
EXCLUSION CRISIS, 1678–1681

It was in this situation that the Popish Plot broke out, a throwback to Tudor times.[1] The principal actor, Titus Oates, the son of a Baptist preacher, was ordained in the Church of England. He was a homosexual who was dismissed as chaplain of the Tangiers garrison owing to over-fondness for the sailors on the way there. Becoming a Roman Catholic, he studied unsuccessfully to become a Jesuit at Valladolid in Spain and at St Omer in France, but he claimed a bogus doctorate in divinity from the celebrated University of Salamanca in Spain. Returning to London, furi-ous at the Jesuits for rejecting him, he met Israel Tongue, a mentally deranged fanatic who maintained in a book no one would publish that the Jesuits had caused the Civil War, the execution of Charles I, and the Great Fire of London in 1666. Some of these stories had been invented earlier by William Prynne, the bitterest opponent of Charles I. This was music to Oates's ears in his mood at the time and it was well adapted for a nonconformist audience. Together they borrowed the lines of former Protestant plots in the reign, in which their relations had been implicated. The plot involved the assassination of the King and of his brother James, Duke of York, with the complicity of Louis XIV and a general rising in which the Presbyterians and the Jesuits were allies. Tongue revealed all this to Charles II, who said he did not believe either Louis XIV or the Jesuits were out to assassinate him. He then left for the Newmarket races, leaving his ministers to deal with the affair. This was a mistake as Danby, who dealt with it, risked being accused of misprison of treason if he did not take the charges seriously. Drawing on the knowledge of prominent

English Catholics his career had given him, Oates took his testimony before Sir Edmund Berry Godfrey, a respected London magistrate. Oates mentioned Edward Coleman, the Duke of York's former secretary and a Catholic convert, who was warned by Godfrey, but foolishly kept his papers. What transformed Oates's unlikely tale into the 'Popish Plot' was the unexplained death of Sir Edmund Berry Godfrey and Danby's decision (and he was no friend of the Duke of York) to seize Coleman's papers. Coleman's letters, written some years previously, talked of extirpating Protestant heresy and converting England to Catholicism. These notions, it should be stressed, were not shared by the Duke of York. On a more practical basis his papers revealed that he had been sent 300 000 crowns by Père Lachaise, Louis XIV's confessor. This was not to assassinate Charles but to distribute, through Coleman, bribes to MPs to prevent a war against France. The death of Godfrey and the discovery of Coleman's papers lent authenticity to Oates's narrative and Oates's talent as a fantasist did the rest. Henry Coventry, the Secretary of State, a man of sense, said either Oates was telling the truth or he was the most accomplished liar he had ever come across. In the years 1678–79 collective hysteria gripped England, akin to *la grande peur* (irrational fears of the enemy within), which led to the Terror during the French Revolution. The most fantastic rumours spread about the small number of Catholics in London being set to murder all Protestants in their beds. Sir Thomas Player, Chamberlain of and MP for London, declared he fully expected to wake up one morning with his throat cut by the Papists! Sir Joseph Williamson, the Secretary of State, wrote privately that since there was only about one Roman Catholic in London to 1000 Protestants, a wholesale massacre of Protestants seemed unlikely, but he kept these doubts to himself. Coleman's execution was speeded up by the Whig MPs who had received bribes from France through him. The plot had taken on a political dimension to exclude James from the throne as a Roman Catholic and to secure power for the Whigs. Prompted by Sir William Waller, MP, the dissolute and bankrupt son of a Parliamentary Civil War commander, Oates accused and identified the men the Whigs wanted to be rid of. Waller went round Westminster seizing objects of 'popish superstition', religious paintings and crucifixes to be burnt in ritual ceremonies, but he kept back and sold valuables among them for his own benefit. Members of Parliament who disbelieved the reality of the plot were expelled or had to recant publicly.[2]

    A hectic two and a half years followed the outbreak of the Popish Plot. The main objects of opponents of the Court were to secure the fall of

Danby as Lord Treasurer and the exclusion of the Duke of York from the royal succession. Danby was impeached as a result of Ralph Montagu's (the most devious politician in an unscrupulous age) revelations that he had been involved in seeking subsidies from France. Fortunately for the King, the terms of the Secret Treaty of Dover of 1670 with Louis were not known. A new Test Act was passed in 1678 which excluded Roman Catholic peers, including the Duke of York, from the Lords as well as a handful of Catholic MPs who sat in the Commons. Under tremendous pressure, Charles stood firm to protect his Queen, Catherine of Braganza, who was accused, as a Roman Catholic, by Oates of complicity in the plot, together with his brother James and Danby. Tempers ran high, especially as the Licensing Act which regulated the press had expired and the violence of the Whig press was unchecked. Petitions and instructions to MPs were printed, all furthering the Whig cause, in tactics later copied repeatedly.[3] There followed the three Exclusion Parliaments of 1679, 1680 and 1681 in which the Whigs carried all before them in elections, not only in prestigious large constituencies, such as London and Westminster, but in the corporation boroughs where the Dissenters had remained entrenched. The Court did not intervene in the elections and thus spent no money on them. In contrast, winning the elections, particularly in the venal boroughs, was very expensive for opponents of the Court. Shaftesbury, the most influential of the popular Whig leaders at this time, put forward a scheme for a franchise of freeholders in all boroughs, a proposal taken up by reformers at the end of the eighteenth century. Failing to convince the Lords who rejected the Second Exclusion Bill in 1680 or to exclude the bishops from the Upper House, the Exclusionists talked not of respect for the royal prerogative but of their responsibility for 'the People' and condemned all opponents as popishly affected. The great positive achievement of the First Exclusion Parliament was the passing of the Habeas Corpus Act in 1679, which prevented arbitrary imprisonment without trial and became regarded as a fundamental part of the unwritten constitution.

In the great Pope- and Devil-burning ceremonies, bishops were burnt in effigy without distinguishing between Catholic and Anglican bishops.[4] The newly raised regiments were disbanded in 1679–80, leaving Charles with only his personal guard. The Whigs passed a bill to call out the militia, which brought back memories and fears of 1641 and the Civil War. The King used his veto against it, the only time he had vetoed a Parliamentary bill.[5] The Whigs had believed they could force Charles to accept his brother's exclusion from the throne. The King agreed to the proposals of the Marquess of Halifax, 'the Great Trimmer', to place limitations on James's power when he succeeded, but never to Exclusion. He foiled his enemies by repeatedly dissolving and proroguing Parliament. Using his great powers of dissimulation to good use, he gave the Exclusionists enough rope to hang themselves. He sent James into exile and then put him in charge of Scotland, where he made himself popular and strengthened the position of the monarchy and his own as heir the Crown.[6] The weakness of the Whigs was that they had no credible alternative to James as successor. Shaftesbury had become intimate with the Duke of Monmouth, one of Charles II's natural sons, who was handsome and popular, but the King repeatedly and publicly denied Monmouth's claim that Charles had married Monmouth's mother, Lucy Walter, while in exile. London juries, selected by Whig sheriffs, pricked (selected) all Whig juries, which protected Shaftesbury and others from prosecution. Shaftesbury even attempted to get the Middlesex Grand Jury to present the Duke of York as a recusant and the Duchess of Portsmouth, the king's favourite mistress, as a common prostitute.[7] Belief in the Popish Plot began to wane and the Irish evidences began to turn against their Whig paymasters and to testify for the Court. The 1st Duke of Ormonde, as Lord Lieutenant of Ireland, had managed to keep Ireland quiet, and Shaftesbury's attempt to revive the flagging Popish Plot by exporting it to Ireland failed, though it resulted in the execution of Oliver Plunkett, Archbishop of Armagh. Oates had cost the lives of over 30 innocent people, mainly priests, who were executed simply because they were priests. Only one of the Roman Catholic peers accused by Oates, Viscount Stafford,was put to death. Ironically enough, he had earlier supported the Whigs.

3

THE TORY REACTION, 1683–1686

The Anglican clergy were forthright in defending the monarchy and the Duke of York's title. Alarmed by popular disorders, the Tory Anglican reaction gained strength rapidly, as 'abhorrers' expressed their disapproval at the attacks being made on the royal prerogative. With the brilliant assault of Dryden (himself a Catholic convert) on Shaftesbury and the Whigs in *Absalom and Achitopel* (1681) and Sir Roger L'Estrange's Tory campaign in newspapers and pamphlets, the Court began to win the propaganda war. London was the chief hurdle for the Court, with the Livery (the major City companies or guilds) unpurged of Dissenters, choosing Whig MPs and sheriffs who impanelled all Whig juries. The London apprentices, however, who had been boldest in calling for the Restoration in 1660, began to espouse the King's cause once again.[1] Sir George Jeffreys, who had been Recorder of London and originally an opponent of the Court, but who had rallied to the King, thought of a very ingenious scheme. The office of Sheriff of London was extremely expensive and the City of London had raised money by choosing wealthy Londoners known to be loath to serve and who would opt to pay a fine instead. The way this was done was not by electing the Sheriffs by the Livery in Common Hall, the normal way of choosing Sheriffs, but by the Lord Mayor selecting one Sheriff at the Bridgehouse feast by sending the mayoral cup to one or several hapless London freemen, who had to pay a large fine in order to avoid serving the office. Sir Robert Clayton did this three times as Lord Mayor. Sir John Moore, a Tory Lord Mayor chosen as the alderman next in the chair according to custom, sent the cup to Dudley North, a wealthy London merchant from a politically influential family and, as prearranged, he agreed to serve as Sheriff. All hell broke loose, but the stranglehold of the Whigs over the City had been broken. All this had been done under close guidance from the King. The sacramental test was then imposed on the Livery. The day after Peter Rich, another Tory, was elected Sheriff, Shaftesbury fled abroad. Legal proceedings known as *quo warranto* followed, asking by what right the City of London enjoyed its liberties, which resulted in the confiscation of the London charter and the remodelling of a new one.[2] Many such proceedings in all parts of the country ensued, remodelling the corporations in the Tory interest, often at the behest of local Tory squires, with the Crown having the right to name officers in the new charters, which often granted new privileges to boroughs. The Tory reaction involved stricter application of recusancy laws against Dissenters as well as Roman Catholics. Dissenters who became occasional conformists by taking the Sacrament once a year in order to qualify for office, were often excommunicated. Hardest hit were the Quakers, because they refused to pay tithes and because their refusal to swear oaths often led them to be thrown into prison, charged with contempt of court.

Angered by Louis XIV's acquisition of Strasbourg in 1681, William of Orange urged Charles to come to terms with Parliament, which angered the King. Whether as a ploy or in earnest, Charles told Louis he would call a Parliament if the Treaty of Nijmegen (1679) was violated by France. The fact that Louis had settled to retain fewer towns than all those he had captured was largely due to the substantial forces Charles had sent to the Low Countries.[3] Neither Louis nor Charles wanted war, which was fortunate, as peace brought increasing revenue from the Customs, and with this an adequate revenue for the King and commercial prosperity for his subjects. These were King Charles's golden days, as they were celebrated in retrospect. When James returned to England in 1682, he was widely welcomed, in London especially.

In desperation Whig extremists devised the Rye House Plot. Part of the plan was to assassinate Charles II and his brother James, as they made they way back to London from the Newmarket races in early April 1683. The place chosen was Captain Rumbold's house, The Rye, near Hoddesdon in Hertfordshire, where the road narrowed and offered cover for the conspirators. Robert Ferguson, one of the plotters, sought to recruit 'fierce bigoted men of Religion who were under an invincible fear of Popery' for the task. The attempt was linked with plans for a general rising and the seizure of the Tower of London directed by the Council of Six, which consisted of men of a higher social rank. The assassination miscarried as there was a fire at Newmarket which caused Charles and

James to leave early, but the plan was betrayed to the government by one of the conspirators. A sign that the plotters meant business is that the London Whigs imprisoned the Tory aldermen in Skinners Hall for a day at the crucial time.[4] Monmouth confessed to the truth of the conspiracy and the share in it of William, Lord Russell, son of the Earl of Bedford, a prominent MP and a member of the Council of Six. This sealed the fate of Algernon Sidney, a distinguished republican thinker, who was also a member of the Council of Six. Monmouth recanted once pardoned by Charles.[5] Others involved, such as John Hampden, paid not with their lives but with heavy fines, £40 000 in Hampden's case. He could not pay so he remained in prison.[6]

After the dissolution of the 1681 Parliament, leading opponents of the Court had lost their parliamentary privilege. Sir William Waller fled to Holland to escape imprisonment at the request of his creditors, returning to England with William of Orange in 1688. In June 1683 the judges declared the London charter forfeit and the livery companies followed suit by surrendering their charters. The livery was regulated. Wholesale surrender or confiscation of charters followed and corporations were remodelled in the Tory interest, often in the initiative of Tory gentry. It has been assumed that Charles never meant to call another Parliament, but these measures would have given the Court a majority and we cannot assume that he was resolved to rule without Parliament. However, provided he did not go to war, his revenue was now adequate. He avoided headlong conflict with his subjects by a deathbed conversion to Roman Catholicism in 1685. The King's exile in Catholic countries would have given him a more realistic view of that religion than that held by many of his subjects. By leaving his conversion to the end, he avoided many difficulties. The conversion was nevertheless sincere, as he received the sacraments from Father Huddleston, the same priest who had helped him escape after the Battle of Worcester in 1651. Halifax, a hostile witness, commented: 'those who saw him die saw a very great deal'.[7] Like the Emperor Constantine, the first Christian Emperor, he sought to wipe the slate clean and by a deathbed conversion to be purged of all his sins at the last.

4

JAMES II'S REIGN, MONMOUTH'S REBELLION, TOLERATION FOR ALL, AND THE ANGLICAN BACKLASH

Charles II had left the Crown in an exceptionally strong position. The accession of James II, who had been publicly known as a Roman Catholic since 1673, was not questioned by the Tory majority in the country. The head of the Church of England, a Church for which his grandfather Charles I had died in 1649, did not believe Anglicanism was the true faith and the sole road to eternal salvation. It was a personal wrench for James, too, as hitherto he had been closest to his two brothers-in-law, Henry Hyde, 2nd Earl of Clarendon and Lawrence Hyde, lst Earl of Rochester (whose sister Anne Hyde was James's first wife), and William Sancroft, Archbishop of Canterbury. Yet while Catholicism remained the King's private religion, most people accepted the situation. James levied the Customs and Excise duties before he had been granted them by Parliament to meet the expense of crushing the Monmouth rebellion of 1685, but this was later legalised by the 1685 Parliament, which granted them to him for life, as his brother had them. This left James in a comfortable financial position.[1] The scale of the Monmouth rebellion, consisting of Dissenters and Whig supporters mainly in the lower social scale, was astonishing as they outnumbered James's army. They comprised a motley crew, including Daniel Defoe, Lord Delamer, and Isaac Manley of the Post Office. Members of the great Whig landed families, such as the Whartons and the Hampdens, did not take part, nor did the firebrand John Wildman, who had been a Leveller. The Dutch allowed Monmouth to make his preparations on their soil, but William of Orange gave him no help. Lord Feversham, the commander-in-chief, and the King's army stood firm and defeated Monmouth.[2] The penalties for rising in arms under the laws of treason were savage (hanging, drawing and quartering), no less so than in crushing the Jacobite risings in 1716 or 1746 (when fewer prisoners were sentenced) than in 1685. The Bloody Assizes at Taunton, presided over by Judge Jeffreys, dealt out massive penalties, death or transportation, but caused public opprobrium only as part of Whig mythology after 1689.

Jeffreys was in a different, jocular, mood when he presided over the trial of Titus Oates for perjury, also in 1685. It was the most fashionable spectacle in London and caused much mirth. Collective amnesia had struck those who had supported Oates's testimony during the Exclusion crisis. Only the Earl of Huntingdon, a Whig peer who later became a Jacobite, was truthful enough to declare he had believed Titus Oates but he now thought he was a great liar. Oates was sentenced to be flogged from the Aldgate to Newgate and from Newgate to Tyburn, but he was tough and he survived. Charles II had stopped the pension awarded to him during Exclusion and he became a Baptist preacher.[3]

The elections to the 1685 Parliament were a triumph for the Court; even London returned four Tories. Most probably because of the Monmouth rebellion, James had begun to increase the strength of his army and this led to differences with even some of the most loyal Royalists. Nevertheless, James was accepted as the legitimate king by the Tory majority in the nation, as well as Dissenters and Roman Catholics. James received a Vicar-Apostolic for England, four Catholic bishops were appointed and he received a Papal Nuncio in 1687, but he was careful never to grant any former monastic land to Roman Catholics. For the first time since the reign of Mary Tudor, mass was said publicly in the Chapel Royal at St James's designed by Wren, and attended by some Anglican courtiers and political Catholic converts, such as the 2nd Earl of Sunderland. Many more, however, attended Princess Anne's Anglican Chapel in Whitehall.[4]

James II, like his co-religionists, subsequently became the universal scapegoat, and the majority of historians cannot mention his name without condemning him first. He ended the monopoly of office of the Church of England, the staunchest supporters of the Crown, which was politically unwise. But can we condemn him for giving toleration and civil rights to Protestant Dissenters, Roman Catholics and Jews? The Anglicans, who had been looking forward to consolidating their hegemony in Church and State, were in for a rude shock in the years 1687–88. James alienated his Tory natural supporters. The First Declaration of Indulgence in April 1687 deprived the Church of England of its established status, while the Second Declaration in 1688 gave only limited safeguards to the Church of England. Dissenters and Roman Catholics were admitted to commissions of the peace, the militia, commissions in the army and navy and places in the universities. Many historians have assumed that granting toleration to Protestant Dissenters was a mere ploy to admit fellow Roman Catholics to office.[5] It is true to say that James had not previously advocated toleration. He had been brought up as a High Anglican and supported Clarendon, the father of his first wife Anne Hyde (who became a Catholic herself). He imposed Episcopalian uniformity in Scotland in the 1680s and crushed the Cameronians, who rebelled there, which no doubt encouraged Tories to think he would continue Anglican hegemony.[6] He favoured the Tory reaction of the 1680s in England, too. His later conversion to the rightness of toleration and his conviction that none should be persecuted for their religious beliefs was genuine, however. On his accession he released large numbers of Quakers from prison and he formed a close friendship with William Penn, the founder of Pennsylvania, who believed freedom of worship was a basic right and who was consulted on religious policies. In 1686 Penn was sent to ask Mary, James's daughter and heir, and her husband, William of Orange, to consent to the repeal of the Test Acts and Penal Laws. They agreed to the non-enforcement of the Penal Laws but not to the repeal of the Tests.[7] Penn, knowing that James's belief in toleration was genuine, remained a Jacobite for many years after the Revolution of 1689, was arrested eight times on charges of high treason, and quakers visited James in exile in France. While he was in exile at Saint-Germain-en-Laye, James had a Baptist called Roberts as his secretary and Dennis Granville (the former Dean of Durham and Lord Bath's brother) as his Anglican chaplain. The exiled King practised toleration within the constraints imposed by his host, Louis XIV, which shows he believed in the rightness of toleration in itself.[8]

The vast majority of the aristocracy and gentry, when consulted on the repeal of the Test Acts and Penal Laws, refused to agree. It was a consultative exercise and it most probably represented the majority view. James's alliance with Nonconformists was as objectionable to Tories as his help to Roman Catholics. Historians have, therefore, assumed that James's policies were unworkable. Yet they were devised by James's chief minister, the 2nd Earl of Sunderland, a former Whig and the most astute politician of the day. J. R. Jones first noticed that the policy of looking to the Dissenters and former Whigs to obtain a pliant Parliament was a realistic option. The unreformed House of Commons was elected on a system of inverse proportional representation. As Sir William Petyt calculated, in the counties 160 000 freeholders returned only 91 MPs, while in the boroughs about 40 000 electors returned 418 MPs.[9] The work of the History of Parliament has shown that, apart from London, most Protestant Nonconformists at the lower social levels especially, co-operated enthusiastically with James II. The exceptions were the great Presbyterian families, such as the Whartons, the Hampdens, the Harleys and the Foleys. For instance, at Lyme Regis, a stronghold of Monmouth's in 1685, John Burridge, a Dissenter who became a Whig MP in 1689, carried the town in voting for an address in favour of the 1687 Declaration of Indulgence and pledged support in choosing 'right men' for James's proposed new Parliament in 1688. A Lancashire Dissenter wrote that he and his co-religionists welcomed 'the free and open exercise of their religion' but that it 'much affronted the bishops and the clergy'.[10] In his hurry to change the political scene, James and his agents acted not only tactlessly but inefficiently, in Devon and Cornwall especially, where the majority of rotten boroughs (corrupt boroughs with a small electorate) were. His agents removed Anglicans and packed corporations (using the powers granted him by the remodelled charters of 1683–85) and local commissions with Dissenters and Roman Catholics with such speed it was difficult to know at times who was in or out.[11] James believed that toleration of Dissenters was right in itself and that, as they numbered so many merchants and small traders, it would be good for commerce as it had been in the United Provinces (the Dutch Republic). James's object at this time was to try and ensure that religious toleration continued in the reign of a Protestant successor.

Historians have questioned the legality of the dispensing power to suspend the operation of the Test Acts and Penal Laws, so much condemned after 1689, yet the majority of the judges declared it legal and the judges decided what was law. James has been represented as seeking to establish absolutism (unrestricted government) as well as Roman Catholicism as the state religion. Some commentators, not understanding the vital importance of religion in the seventeenth century, have seen, wrongly, James's toleration in purely political terms as a means of subjecting Parliament and creating an absolute monarchy.[12] The Church of England, the religion of the vast majority of people in England, kept its patronage, churches and cathedrals, but it ceased to be the only recognised church. James was doing in the late seventeenth century what was done at the beginning of the nineteenth century, a revolutionary king faced with a conservationist reaction. James did not aim at the forcible conversion of England to Roman Catholicism. What he wanted was to put his Roman Catholic co-religionists on an equal footing with Anglicans, to enable them to worship in public, to send their sons to the universities of Oxford and Cambridge and to hold employment under the state and in the armed forces. He did not, as the Bill of Rights stated, seek to subvert and extirpate the Protestant religion.[13] The speed with which his policies were forced through was probably dictated by a wish to give protection to Catholics and toleration to all before his daughter Mary succeeded to the throne. The Anglican clergy had preached divine hereditary right and non-resistance, but, to the concern of James, would not practise it. James placed the Anglicans in a terrible quandary. The Fellows of Magdalen College, Oxford, saw it as a violation of their privileges and their property rights when in 1687 the King called upon them to elect Anthony Farmer, a recent convert to Catholicism, as their president, and proceeded to choose John Hough, an Anglican, instead. After several months, this election was declared void by the Ecclesiastical Commission. Samuel Parker, Catholic Bishop of Oxford, was installed as president and the Fellows of Magdalen were 'deprived and expelled'.[14] They regarded themselves as Christian martyrs. The Anglican case was 'to disobey unrighteous sovereigns but never to rebel', and preferred to call this 'non-assistance' rather than resistance.[15]

In December 1687 James's wife, Mary Beatrice of Modena, was confirmed as pregnant and, if her baby survived (she had had miscarriages in the past) and was male, it would ensure the Catholic succession. Not waiting until the birth, Mary's husband, William of Orange, and the United Provinces began preparations for invading England,[16] unbeknownst to James or the English in general. The birth of the Prince of Wales on 10 June 1688 was seen by James and Mary Beatrice as heaven-sent. It was witnessed by the Court, as was the custom, by Lord and Lady Sunderland and others,[17] and was greeted by loyal addresses from most parts of the country. The Prince of Wales was baptised as a Roman Catholic. The Prince of Orange sent congratulations at first, but soon changed tack. The warming-pan story, that the Prince of Wales was a supposititious child, smuggled into the Queen's bed in a warming-pan, seems have originated in Holland. It was meant to strike a blow at the legitimacy of the royal line and to enable William to press the claim to the Crown of his wife Mary and his own as if nothing new had happened. More cruel than Herod, Dean Granville of Durham argued, the Prince of Orange sought to brand 'a hopeful young prince' his nephew as illegitimate and to disinherit him.[18] The story, however absurd, was believed by those whose interest it was to believe it, including Princess Anne, James's second daughter, who purposely did not attend the birth. John Ashton, clerk of the closet to Mary Beatrice, an Anglican and later a Nonjuror (one who refused to take the oaths to William and Mary), collected the evidence of 60 Protestant eye-witnesses of the birth (Roman Catholics were deemed not to be reliable witnesses) to present at the enquiry the Prince of Orange had promised into the birth, which was never held. Ashton was executed as a Jacobite in 1690, presumably to silence him.[19]

The other great case of resistance to James's authority was that of the Seven Bishops. In May 1688 Sancroft, Archbishop of Canterbury, and six bishops petitioned the King, begging to be excused from reading the Second Declaration of Indulgence in their churches as the dispensing power had been declared illegal by Parliament. The petition was widely publicised and the result was that the King's order to read the Declaration in all churches was widely ignored, 95 per cent of the clergy refusing to read it. Their refusal, it was said, was because 'all religion would be let in, be they what they will, Ranter, Quaker, and the like, nay, even the Roman Catholic religion (as they call it)'.[20] James saw this as 'a standard of rebellion'. Sunderland did all he could, but failed to dissuade James from prosecuting the Seven Bishops.[21] The King did not take the case to the Ecclesiastical Commission but to the King's Bench as a seditious libel, which made it a common-law case.[22] It was a complete reversal of the principle *cuius regio eius religio* ('the religion of the ruler determines that of the kingdom'), which prevailed over Europe since the sixteenth century. Defending the bishops was John Somers, a talented Whig lawyer, who argued that there was nothing seditious in the petition because 'the intent was innocent'. The judges were divided and referred the matter to a jury who, on 30 June, returned a verdict of not guilty, amidst scenes of great popular rejoicing.[23] These events have been regarded by some historians as leading inexorably to the Glorious Revolution, but the Seven Bishops did not want to bring in William of Orange. Five out of the seven would not recognise William as king in 1689 and most of them plotted to bring back James thereafter.[24] Tory crowds celebrated the acquittal of the Seven Bishops, whom they saw as trying to protect them against Nonconformity, as well as against Roman Catholicism. They vented their anger against the house of the Earl of Salisbury, a prominent Roman Catholic convert.[25] The High Anglicans, apart from Danby's friend, Compton, Bishop of London, sought to persuade James to change tack and revert to support for Anglican hegemony, but did not seek to dethrone him. Nevertheless, had it not been for foreign intervention, people would have lived with James's measures, which were moderate, though tactlessly and sometimes brutally imposed.

It has been thought that James's religious policies were modelled on Louis XIV's. This was not the case. James's policies differed radically from those of Louis XIV, who persecuted the Huguenots and tried to convert them to Catholicism by force. James had disapproved of the Revocation of the Edict of Nantes (which ended the toleration and special privileges Henry IV had granted the Huguenots in the sixteenth century). James said the Revocation was neither Christian nor wise, as he told the Spanish and Dutch envoys. He had, in fact, welcomed the Huguenots and given them their first church in Soho Fields.[26] After the Revolution they, like other Protestant Dissenters, with the exception of the Quakers, proved James's and Louis's bitterest enemies. James did not seek and could not have obtained absolute power. Nor did James plan to rule without Parliament, for his policies were to remodel corporations and local commissions so as to secure a Parliament that would repeal the Test Act and Penal Laws. It was condemned as illegal after the Revolution. Was it less so than the vast system of corruption and patronage, relying on those same boroughs, which produced the solid phalanx of placemen and pensioners doing the Court's bidding in Parliament and which ensured that eighteenth-century governments did not lose a general election, even if the majority of votes cast had been for the opposition?

One aspect of James's reign has usually been glossed over: sound management of the country's finances. He practised retrenchment by cutting the size of his Household but paying its members regularly. The Earl of Rochester, his Lord Treasurer, was one of the very few holders of the office who did not enrich himself at public expense. The army, the navy and government officials were paid regularly and, unlike Charles II and William III, James left virtually no debts. The High Tories,who had supervised financial reforms earlier in the reign, headed by Rochester and Clarendon, together with Sancroft, Archbishop of Canterbury and Bishop Turner, kept up pressure on James to reverse his policy of religious toleration. With the looming threat of a Dutch invasion, they succeeded. Sunderland was dismissed and High Anglicans, such as Lord Preston and Lord Middleton, who had managed the 1685 Parliament for James, were back in office as Secretaries of State. Samuel Johnson, a Williamite Whig clergyman, was so infuriated by this High Tory success that he complained they 'intended to forestal [sic] our expected deliverance'.[27] James's Declaration of September 1688 had returned all corporations to their pre-1679 state, thus undoing his brother's remodelling of charters and his own packing of corporations since 1687. These measures excluded Roman Catholics once more, but had the result of leaving Dissenters in control of as many corporations as they had at the time of the Exclusion crisis. Whether James intended this, or whether it was generally regarded as a return to past practice, is not clear. It is a crucial document, however, because as party disputes after 1689 made it impossible to pass a new Corporation Act, it remained the settlement in force.

5

THE INTERNATIONAL COALITION AGAINST FRANCE AND THE DUTCH INVASION

On 30 June 1688, 20 days after the birth of the Prince of Wales, a group of peers known to history as 'the Immortal Seven' – Lords Shrewsbury, Devonshire, Danby and Lumley, Bishop Compton, Edward Russell and Henry Sydney, all Whigs except Danby and his friend Compton – sent the Prince an Invitation to come to England, with the signatures in code only because of fears of disclosure. It could be interpreted as inviting William to come over to restrain James but not necessarily to displace the King. They were a small group and a not particularly representative one, but it gave William the pretext he needed. In fact the preparations for William's expedition had begun in April 1688, before the birth of the Prince of Wales.[1] A small group of army officers led by John, Lord Churchill, the Duke of Grafton, Percy Kirke and Charles Trelawny, some of whom belonged to the Anglo-Dutch regiments or to the Tangiers garrison, took part in what is known as the Army Plot and began to act in collusion with William before the invasion. They were at first little more than an intelligence-gathering organisation and a debating club, and did not act in earnest until the successful Dutch invasion. In the summer of 1688 Englishmen had no love for the Dutch and there was no general movement to oust James or a groundswell of opinion in favour of the Prince of Orange. When the Whig Henry Sidney, son of the Earl of Leicester, arrived at the Hague in July 1688 he said:

he could not believe what they suggested concerning the king's army being disposed to come over to him, nor did he reckon, as much as they did, on the people of the country coming in to him; he said he could trust to neither of these. He could not undertake so great a design, the miscarriage of which would be the ruin of England and Holland, without such a force as he had reason to believe would be superior to the king's own, though his whole army should stick to him.

James had but vague and uncritical reports from the Marquis d'Albeville, his envoy at the Hague, and he could not bring himself to believe that his 'nephew and son-in-law could be capable of so ill an undertaking'.[2] James, moreover, misunderstood the nature of the international crisis developing in 1688. France posed no real threat to England or any part of the British Isles. James was neither the ally nor a client of Louis XIV and his policy had been to keep Britain and Europe at peace. As Stadholder, William had little power in the Dutch Netherlands, where he was regarded as the head of the anti-democratic party, in Amsterdam especially. Amsterdam believed religious toleration was good for trade and allowed Roman Catholics to worship privately, though not to hold office. The Prince, however, was also, significantly, Captain-General of the United Provinces, and he capitalised on fears there of the power of France. Jonathan Israel has revealed the extent to which the invasion was planned and paid for by the Dutch States General, Amsterdam, the Regents, and a group of urban patricians who ran the Dutch States. They and William had been building up a vast coalition against France in which they enlisted Catholic powers, the Emperor Leopold I especially, and had support from the King of Spain and diplomatic support from the Pope, Innocent XI, all of whom had scores to settle with Louis XIV. Louis was presented as seeking universal monarchy, but in reality his conquests in terms of territory and population were trivial compared to those of Leopold I (Holy Roman Emperor 1657–1705), Charles VI (Holy Roman Emperor 1711–40), or Peter the Great of Russia (Tsar 1689–1725).[3] The Prince of Orange gave the Rulers in the Coalition assurances that he would respect the lawful succession in England, protect Catholics and get the Test Acts repealed. William's failure to keep any of these promises was to lead to recriminations from his allies. It was Louis XIV's past aggressions, and recently the war of the *Réunions*, by which he had forcibly annexed Strasbourg and other towns in 1683–84, that had built up the coalition against him. The irony of it is that he was not preparing for a major war in 1688. His military strategy, then, was essentially defensive: building fortresses to protect the more easily defended French frontiers he had acquired in the North and East. There was no increase in the size of his peacetime

army.[4] In September 1688 he was besieging Philippsburg, a fortress on
the Rhine crucial to the defence of Alsace. The French fleet had been sent
to the Mediterranean and could not have blocked the Dutch invasion
even if asked to do so by James. All these events enabled William of
Orange to seize the English throne.[5]

The Revolution of 1688–89 should be seen in the context of European
history, rather than as a purely British affair. Yet the Prince of Orange
was able to project himself as the defender of Protestantism against the
Roman Catholic powers, who were often perceived as having relegated
the Protestant states to the periphery of Europe. Then and later William
claimed to lead a Protestant crusade, his aim being 'that England should
always make itself the head and protection of the whole Protestant
interest. . . . By making all true Protestants, i.e. all true Christians, her
friends, she enabled England to make good her oldest maxim of state
which was to keep the balance of power of Europe equal and steady.'
William, however, failed to get Denmark and Sweden, leading Protestant
states, as his allies.[6] The preparations on land and sea were massive and
James's ambassador at The Hague reported that the Dutch intended an
'absolute conquest of England'.[7] James was not the ally of Louis XIV and,
having rejected Louis's earlier offers of help, the French armies were tied
up in the Rhineland at the time of the Dutch invasion. The Revolution
has been looked at in the past mainly in English terms. The Dutch States
and their European allies and supporters wished to bring English naval
and military power to bear in a war against France, not to defend the
rights of Parliament or of the Church of England. The Prince of Orange
sought the Crown from the first as he had to be in control of the armed
forces to achieve his purpose. Amphibious operations are notoriously
difficult and William and his forces were dispersed by storms on 27 Octo-
ber 1688. Undeterred, another expedition was mounted. In the words of
a leading naval historian: 'James's loss of his throne in 1688 was not due
to the discontent of some clergymen with troubled consciences, nor to
the plots of provincial noblemen, nor even to the schemes of certain
ambitious army officers. James fell because William was able to land.'
James's fleet was commanded by George Legge, Earl of Dartmouth. He
had been at odds with Arthur Herbert, who had defected to the Dutch,
and he detested John Churchill, James's favourite army officer and the
future Duke of Marlborough. Many naval officers resented the introduction of a few Roman Catholic officers in the navy, but Dartmouth was a
close friend of Sir Roger Strickland, a Roman Catholic convert and a
high-ranking officer in the navy. Dartmouth refused James's request to

carry the Prince of Wales over to France for safety, but his loyalty to the King was never in doubt and he died later in the Tower of London, where he was imprisoned as a Jacobite. The practice at that time was often for officers to hold commissions in the navy as well as in the army. The Duke of Grafton, one such, who was active in the Army Plot, brought about eight naval officers, including Captain Matthew Aylmer and Lieutenant George Byng, into the Orangist conspiracy. Naval officers, however, could not take their ships to the other side as easily as army officers could their troops, as it would have needed all the other naval officers, as well as the crew, to agree to do so. This was as much an obstacle in 1688 as it was in the case of Jacobite naval officers subsequently. Dartmouth knew that William's fleet was superior to his own. He had poor intelligence and he thought that the Dutch would land in Yorkshire or Suffolk. The very east winds which carried William's fleet to the south-west trapped Dartmouth's fleet behind a sandbank, so that he could not intercept the Dutch.[8] Thus it was that the Dutch invasion successfully landed at Torbay and Brixham in Devon during the night and the morning of 4–5 November 1688, symbolically enough, as the 5th was the anniversary of the Gunpowder Plot and the birthday of the Prince of Orange. The Dutch had 463 vessels and 40 000 troops, more than the Spanish Armada of 1588 and much more than the token army of 10 000–15 000 depicted by Macaulay and other historians. It was in fact twice the size of James's army, which was dispersed all over the British Isles.[9] Subsequently, myth replaced reality on the circumstances in which the Prince of Orange set foot on English soil. The statue of William of Orange erected at Torbay in 1888 depicts a local fisherman carrying the Prince ashore, but since there seems no contemporary record of his existence nor of his being rewarded for his feat afterwards, the story seems to be a nineteenth-century invention.

We can merely guess the feelings of various sections of the population as this vast army marched to Exeter: Dutch, many mercenaries, Brandenburgers, Greeks, Swiss, Poles, Swedes, Hessians, Finlanders in bearskins and black slaves from the Dutch plantations. According to Robert Ferguson, William's Presbyterian chaplain, there were more Roman Catholics in William's army than in James's, though others thought the numbers were equal. Heneage Finch, a leading Tory MP, pointed out: 'we have had free quarters constrained almost in all places where the Dutch army have marched. We have in great part a Popish army too, though that was one of the most crying offences we objected to the king.'[10] James told his Dutch gaoler at Rochester that, ' in his whole army of eighteen thousand men, he believed he had not a thousand Roman Catholics, whereas your army ... hath two thirds of my religion so cried out against'.[11] They carried banners with the motto: 'For the defence of the Protestant religion and the Liberty and Property of the subjects of England'. The Prince's First Declaration, which had been drawn up by Gaspar Fagel, a leading figure in the States of Holland, was translated into English by Gilbert Burnet.[12] It was printed in the Netherlands and thousands of copies were dispersed in England shortly before the invasion. It was a skilful piece of propaganda, depicting the Prince as a selfless deliverer bent only on rescuing the nation's religion, laws and liberties from a tyrant – James II – guided by the Jesuits and Louis XIV. Similar broadsides were sent to the officers of the English army and navy.[13] William's Declarations, which were read aloud as they went, crucially denied any design on the Crown and asserted that his expedition was 'intended for no other design, but to have a free and lawful parliament assembled as soon as possible' and to refer to, among other matters, 'the inquiry into the birth of the pretended Prince of Wales ... and to the right of succession'.[14] James's Declaration of 28 September 1688 countered this: 'although some false pretences relating to Liberty, Property, and Religion contrived and worded with art and subtlety, may be given out ... it is manifest, however, (considering the great preparations that are making) that no less matter than by this invasion is proposed than an absolute conquest of these our kingdoms'.[15]

Not everyone was taken in by the Prince of Orange's assurances. William had tried to build up support in the West Country as early as January 1688 when Sir William Waller wrote from Holland to his brother-in-law, Sir William Courtenay of Powderham, who had been an Exclusionist, with assurances that the Prince's only concerns were 'the Protestant interest and the welfare of poor England', and a claim that James was trying to get Mary his daughter divorced from William to get her to 'marry elsewhere'. Courtenay did not reply. Though Dutch propaganda sources depict him as assisting the invasion in November, he ordered his tenants not to join the invaders.[16] All the aldermen of Exeter but one stood by James, though they were unable to withstand William's army. The money collected for the Excise in Exeter and Devon was seized in William's name and continued to be seized in other parts of the country as the advance proceeded. This was all the more remarkable as James, having collected the Excise before being granted it by the 1685 Parliament, was one of the grievances in the Declaration of Rights. Far from welcoming the Prince of Orange, the Bishop and the Dean of Exeter had left before he arrived, as had the gentry and substantial citizens. When Dr Burnet, the Prince's chaplain, held a service in the cathedral, none of the canons were in their stalls and, when he tried to read the Prince's Declaration, the choristers walked out. The preaching of Divine Hereditary Right and non-resistance by Tory Anglican clerics, Burnet thought, had done their work too well. Many of the common people attending an annual fair, however, welcomed the Prince and came to look at him and his army as a peep-show. William suspended the Tory alderman and began steps to remodel the Exeter charter. In ten days no one of any standing had joined William and, according to some contemporaries, William even thought of going back, though this is unlikely.

In mid-November things began to change: leading Whigs such as Thomas Wharton, Colonel Colchester and Colonel Godfrey joined and then Sir Edward Seymour, a Tory and the greatest electoral magnate in the West, followed by many local gentlemen. At Seymour's suggestion they entered into an Association to protect the Prince and to protect themselves. This is not to say that they wanted to make William king, for as Seymour said: 'all the West went into the Prince of Orange upon his declaration, thinking in a free Parliament to redress all that was amiss', but later suspected 'that the Prince aimed at something else'. William's Declaration that he had no designs on the Crown allayed Tory fears at first, particularly Seymour's, who thought England could not have a Dutch king as England and Holland: 'followed the same mistress, trade'. Worse still from James's point of view was the defection of John Granville, Earl of Bath, from a family whose name was synonymous with royalism, who handed over Plymouth to William.

In the North, Danby, who had been the most active on William's behalf, drawing up lists of supporters or opponents of James and trying to get William to land in Yorkshire, which the Prince had no intention of doing, nor of being so far indebted to one of his subjects. The Duke of Newcastle, Lord-Lieutenant of the three Ridings of Yorkshire, remained faithful to James, but he was tormented by gout and proved indecisive. At a meeting of the Yorkshire militia on 14 November at York, the deputy lieutenants drew up a loyal address and refused to petition for a free Parliament while Dutch troops were on English soil. On the 22nd, at a prearranged signal, an associate of Danby's burst into the hall crying out that 'the Papists had risen and fired at the militia troops', which ended the meeting in disarray. Danby's associates, led by his son Lord Dunblane and Lord Lumley (one of the Seven), rode at the head of about 100 horsemen to the cry of 'a Free Parliament, the Protestant Religion, and no Popery', which brought the city of York over. Danby appealed to the Earl of Chesterfield, a great magnate in the Midlands, misleadingly described in a Dutch printed list of William's supporters as in arms for the Prince, to join them. Chesterfield replied that though he had small obligations to the Court, he had 'a natural aversion to the taking of arms against my king, which the law justly terms designing the death of the King'. This was prophetic, for Danby and Dunblane were to assert again and again that had they known that the Prince of Orange, whom they had so often heard say had no designs on the throne, would insist on taking the Crown, they would have had nothing to do with his enterprise. Danby was not to be treated as powerbroker and on 11 December, the day after James's First Flight, he was ordered by William to disband his forces. In Cheshire Lord Delamer, a conspirator in Monmouth's rising and a bankrupt nobleman on the make, raised the standard for the Prince of Orange and began to collect the excise on his behalf. The efforts of some local Cheshire Tories on James's behalf were negated by the inactivity of Lord Derby, the Lord-Lieutenant, who sat on the fence. Chester was crucial since it controlled movements of troops and ships to and from Ireland. Peter Shakerley, Governor of Chester and Thomas Cartwright, Bishop of Chester, co-operated with Catholic forces, and tried to hold Chester, a strategically important place, for James. They were hampered by wild rumours in mid-December, deliberately circulated, that Irish troops (in fact disbanded by Lord Feversham with the rest of James's army) had burnt down Birmingham and Wolverhampton and were preparing to burn down Sheffield, having killed all Protestants. Sir Christopher Musgrave, on the other hand, secured Carlisle for James, after disarming the Roman Catholics in the garrison, but laid down arms on Lord Feversham's orders after James's First Flight. The role of Lords Delamer, Devonshire and Stamford in taking Derby and Nottingham for William has been well documented,[17] but nine out of ten aristocrats did not lift a finger to help William or defend James.[18]

The Revolution was not bloodless, even in England, for there were bloody skirmishes at Wincanton and Reading. As James prepared to leave for Salisbury on 17 November, he sent his Queen and the Prince of Wales to Portsmouth to seek safety in France. Sancroft, Archbishop of Canterbury, presented a petition to him for a free Parliament to settle grievances and prevent bloodshed. James objected to the word 'free' but promised to call regular Parliaments as soon as he had defeated his enemies, and he asked for prayers for his safety and success.[19] The crunch, if it came, would have come on Salisbury Plain. Lords Feversham and Ailesbury begged James on their knees to order the arrest of the Prince of Denmark (Princess Anne's husband), the 2nd Duke of Ormonde, the Duke of Grafton, Lord Churchill, Kirke, Trelawny and others, but he would not do so.[20] James had been suffering from nosebleeds and was deeply hurt by the desertion of his daughters Mary and Anne. At first he was resolved to give battle, but there were good military reasons why he did not. He had 19 000 troops on the ground as against William's forces of over 21 000,[21] and some of his commanders, John Churchill especially, whose fortune he had made, were about to desert him, and James's council of war was unanimous in recommending they should not engage the Dutch.[22] James suspected Churchill of wanting to kidnap him and hand him over to William.[23] Lord Cornbury, the dissolute and transvestite son of the Earl of Clarendon, was the first to try to take his forces to the Prince, but most of the men and officers would not follow when they found out where they were being taken.[24] This attitude continued, for when part of the army mutinied at Ipswich in 1689, the soldiers cried: 'there is no king but King James', which led to the passing of an annual mutiny bill.[25] Lord Churchill, Lord Berkeley, the Duke of Grafton, Charles II's natural son, and Prince George of Denmark went over to the Prince of Orange. Apart from the treachery of leading army officers, because of the horrors of the Civil Wars, there seemed a resolve on all sides in England not to shed further human blood, and James may have sensed that.

On 27 November, at a meeting in Whitehall attended by many peers, Rochester advised the summoning of a free Parliament, the granting of a free pardon to those in arms against the King, and the appointment of commissioners to go to the Prince of Orange and to leave the rest to the discretion of Parliament. Halifax, Godolphin and Nottingham were appointed to treat with the Prince at Hungerford, asking him not to advance to within 40 miles of London, having had an agreement from James to withdraw his forces from London so that Parliament might meet freely. William pursued delaying tactics, not meeting the commissioners until 8 December and refusing to come to terms. He cleverly prevented any private meeting between the wily Halifax and the indiscreet Burnet in case his real intentions were revealed. Burnet was heard to exclaim: 'How can there be a treaty? The sword is drawn, there is a suppositious child, which must be inquired into.'[26] On 10 December, before he knew of James's departure, William sent orders to Admiral Arthur Herbert, who held a commission in the Dutch, not the English navy, to fly the English flag in attacks on French ships, in order to provoke a war with France.[27] A spurious Third Declaration from the Prince, apparently written by Hugh Speke, a Whig fanatic, was widely circulated at this time, claiming that 'armed Papists' were about to attack Protestants in London and Westminster 'by fire, a sudden massacre or both'. There were rumours that Irish troops were coming to London to cut Protestants' throats. Though some suspected it was a forgery at the time, it provoked panic. James was convinced the Prince of Orange would kill his son, whom he sent with the Queen to France for safety. Probably with the fate of his father in mind (though Mary was said to have secured a promise from the Prince that her father would not be harmed), he decided to join them in France. Before his First Flight on 10 December he cancelled the writs calling a Parliament for 15 January, though some had been sent out already, and threw the Great Seal of England into the Thames as he left, to prevent William usurping his royal prerogative. He would expose himself no longer to 'what I might expect from the ambitious Prince of Orange and the associated rebellious lords' and could not imagine that 'all this undertaking was out of pangs of conscience for the religion and liberties of the people'.[28] He sent orders to Lord Feversham, the commander of his army, not to expose himself and others by 'resisting a foreign army and a poisoned nation', which Feversham interpreted as disbanding his army. As these instructions were read out, eye-witnesses reported: 'many of the soldiers [were] weeping and others trembling with anger whilst they heard the order read'.[29] In the King's absence, law and order broke down, and on 11 December the London sky glowed red from the fires of Roman Catholic chapels and houses being burnt, including that of William's ally, the Spanish ambassador. Some members of the crowd carried sticks with oranges stuck at the end of them to show their support for the Prince. Criminals, thieves and looters infiltrated the mob as rich furniture, plate and money worth £20 000 were carried away from the Spanish ambassador's house off Great Queen Street, where many Catholics had been in the habit of going to hear mass, and the altar plate of the King's Chapel was stolen. The embassies of Venice, Tuscany, Cologne and the Palatinate were similarly attacked. Roman Catholics were 'running into all the holes to hide themselves, weeping and crying for fear of their lives', as most of their Protestant neighbours were too apprehensive to give them shelter. Some disbanded soldiers were said to have joined in the looting.

In response to James's flight and the disorders in London, Rochester summoned a meeting of peers temporal and spiritual who were in London to meet in the Guildhall. Most were Loyalists, but they were opposed by violent Whigs or secret Williamites, who managed to block a call for the return of the King and accused Anglican bishops of 'returning to their vomit of Popery'. The Guildhall Declaration, which was published on 12 December, contained no invitation for William to come and take over the government, as Burnet falsely alleged. An address of the Common Council (councillors elected in each of the wards) of the City of London, drafted by the Whigs, and one from the London lieutenancy promoted by Sir Robert Clayton, a wealthy and influential Whig alderman, however, invited the Prince to come to London. On 12 December the peers moved from the Guildhall to the council chamber in Whitehall and chose Halifax as chairman. More fearful of social disorder than of popery, they called out the militia, ordered the Guards to disperse the rabble and sent cavalry to Somerset House to protect the beleaguered Catharine of Braganza, Charles II's widow, who was a Catholic. James was arrested in Faversham in Kent by overzealous Whig fishermen, who mistook him for Sir Edward Hales, a Roman Catholic who had been involved in a notorious legal test case, much to the annoyance of the Prince of Orange, who did not want the inconvenience of James remaining in England. Four Loyalist peers, Feversham, James's Commander-in-Chief, Middleton, his Secretary of State, Yarmouth as Treasurer of the Household and Ailesbury as Gentleman of his Bedchamber (all High Anglicans) were sent to Faversham to persuade the King to return to Whitehall. Halifax and the Williamites disapproved. James sent a message to William inviting him to a personal conference in London to 'settle the distracted nation'. The Prince did not reply. James was brought back to London on 16 December. Encouraged by large cheering crowds at Blackheath, James passed through the City of London and down the Strand in triumph. From Southwark to Whitehall, as he progressed, 'there was scarce room for the coaches to pass through and the balconies and windows were thronged with loud acclamations beyond whatever was heard of'. These crowds could not have been the same people who sacked Roman Catholic houses, including the Spanish ambassador's residence in London, but there were always a Tory and a Whig crowd. James, who was surprised and touched by the warmth of his reception, met four bishops, Archbishop Lamplugh of York, Turner of Ely, White of Peterborough and Sprat of Rochester, telling them he had made a mistake in employing Roman Catholics and would not do so again. The Prince was mortified by the turn of events, as he had planned to arrive in London on the 18th. At a meeting in Windsor, William consulted four lords who had come over with him from the Netherlands – Shrewsbury, Mordaunt, Macclesfield and Wiltshire – two of the rebels in the North, Delamer and Stamford, two rebels from the King's army, Churchill and

Grafton, two Orangists, North and Carbery, and Halifax, who had come over to the Williamites. They advised that James should leave Whitehall and go to Ham, the Duchess of Lauderdale's house on the Thames.[30] Again taking the initiative, Sir Robert Clayton carried a motion, which was accepted by the Common Council, that the City of London could not guarantee James's safety and thus that he should leave London.[31] Dutch troops entered London at night as planned on the 18th, and the King was taken prisoner by them and treated with great disrespect by Count Solms, William's kinsman. As the bishops and foreign ambassadors came to pay their respects to the King, they found him gone.[32] William was in London, which was surrounded by a large Dutch army for 18 months, English troops, including the Palace guards, having been sent 20 miles away from the capital. Dutch prints depicted the Prince of Orange making a triumphal entry into the City of London greeted by loud acclamations, the ringing of bells and an enthusiastic crowd with oranges at the end of their sticks as a sign of support. The reality is that he went from Knightsbridge to St James's Palace through Hyde Park, to avoid the crowd.[33] James, not allowed to go through London a second time, lest the sight of the King being taken prisoner caused an insurrection, was taken at 1 a.m. to Ham House, conveyed by water and then escorted to Rochester from whence he went into exile, deported from his kingdoms by a foreign army. This undertaking, he had thought all along, was 'only a disguised and designed usurpation'.[34] On 4 January 1689 James wrote to the Privy Council to say he had been obliged to leave his country because he feared being put to death.[35]

Meanwhile Whig lords flocked to William's Court to congratulate him on delivering them 'from Popery and slavery'.[36] On 24 December, Lord Paget proposed that as James's withdrawal was tantamount to legal death, Mary should be declared queen and this was seconded by Compton, Bishop of London. Instead, however, a motion was carried to address the Prince of Orange to take the administration of the government into his own hands. As a result of the City of London taking the initiative on William's behalf, the Common Council (the equivalent of the Commons in the corporation) secured the right to appoint many of the civic officers and to enjoy wide powers of patronage.[37] The Common Council won the right to vote addresses and pass resolutions on behalf of the City of London without getting the approval of the Court of Aldermen, a right taken away by Sir Robert Walpole in 1725. On the 26th a meeting was summoned of the Members of Charles II's Parliaments who were in or around London (excluding members of the Loyalist 1685

Parliament), the Lord Mayor, the aldermen and 50 representatives of the Common Council. They asked the Prince to issue circular letters for calling a Parliament[38] and to take over the responsibility of government, which he did two days later. They were in fact ratifying a fait accompli. To secure the English army and with something resembling contempt, William ordered Lord Churchill and the Duke of Grafton, who had done so much to bring chaos to James's army, to set the disbanded forces in order once more.[39]

6

THE 1689 CONVENTION, THE SETTLEMENT OF THE CROWN AND THE BILL OF RIGHTS

The Prince of Orange had kept everyone guessing about his intentions. Edward Harley wrote: 'the Prince carries all things with that secrecy that few know his mind. . . . It is not known that he spoke to any person or let them know his inclination as to the disposing of the Crown.'[1] Sir Edward Seymour told Clarendon that if the Prince of Orange violated his Declaration and claimed the throne, 'it would be impossible for honest men to believe him' in future. Only Bentinck, William's Dutch mentor, and the Dutch probably knew what Mary did know: that the Prince would settle for nothing but the Crown. Englishmen had to be kept in the dark to prevent a reaction from the Tories who had been duped by William's assurances he had no design on the Crown. Bentinck told Clarendon (James's brother-in-law by James's first wife, Anne Hyde) on 4 December 1688 that 'there are not evil men wanting, who give it out that the Prince aspires at the Crown, which is the most wicked insinuation that could be invented'.[2] Circular letters were sent out to all counties, cities, cinque ports and universities to choose representatives to meet as a Convention at Westminster on 22 January.[3] James's writs calling a new Parliament had been recalled by him on the grounds that there could be no free election while Dutch troops were on English soil. Nevertheless, a mini general election was held on them in several counties, Yorkshire especially, but these returns were disregarded. The writs were sent not to the Sheriffs of each county, as was the common practice, not surprisingly, since they had been pricked by Lord Chancellor Jeffreys in anticipation of James's proposed new Parliament, but to the coroners. The elections were free of pressure from the Prince of Orange himself, but not from pressure by his supporters, one of whom, William Harbord, who came over from Holland in 1688, managed to have himself returned for two boroughs and to secure the nomination of Members for a further two seats.[4] It was usual for county returns to be signed by the leading gentry and in corporation boroughs to have the return signed by the aldermen,. if not by the whole corporation, but most of the 1689 election returns were not so signed, often not even by the returning officer.[5] There were far fewer contests than in the elections in 1690 or even those in 1685. The Convention produced a large Whig majority, which reinforced William's overestimate of the strength of the Whigs in the country at large. According to John Milner, one of its Members, there were 170 Dissenters in the Commons in 1689.[6]

It was not until 26 January 1689 when there was a 'full House', 417 Members, that Commons proceedings began in earnest. All sides rejected the idea of a Commonwealth (a republic) as unacceptable, presumably because of the civil strife associated with it in the past. In law the King never died and a vacancy to the throne could not exist. This is probably why the Whigs were suspicious of Tory references to the ancient constitution (the unwritten constitution, which included, in the eyes of many, an indefeasible right of hereditary succession to the Crown) or to Magna Carta as obstructive. One of the solutions proposed, that of a Regency, was attractive as it obviated any need to tamper with the succession, and James would remain technically on the throne while William exercised his powers. James was not likely to agree, nor would William have been satisfied with this. All sides ignored the existence of the Prince of Wales and his claim, and the promised inquiry into the circumstances of his birth was never held. Danby, the head of what was called the Maryites, argued that the throne should pass to Mary, William's wife, as the next Protestant heir. Some Whigs, on the other hand, argued that James had broken the original contract with the people, and, as he had left the kingdom, the throne was therefore vacant.[7]

The notion of the original contract was the brainchild of John Locke. Locke was a conspirator in the Rye House Plot who fled to Holland in 1683 and returned with William of Orange in 1688. He did not as yet enjoy his subsequent reputation as one of the greatest thinkers of the time, as he did not publish his two *Treatises on Government* until August 1689. In these, Locke argued that William (he did not mention Mary) owed the Crown to the choice of the people, the only foundation of lawful government.[8] He defended the right to rebel and to prevent as well as to resist tyranny. An Arian (one who denied the divinity of Christ), Locke wanted a separation of Church and State, writing in his *Letter on Toleration* that the business of true religion was to regulate men's lives in accordance with virtue and piety. He would have granted limited toleration to the Church of England and none at all to the Roman Catholics.[9] His writings were badly received at the time. The doctrine of the social contract was dynamite, as it would enable the people to remove and replace other kings or queens in future. It was unacceptable to William and it was omitted from the Declaration of Rights. The Whigs insisted afterwards and for the rest of the eighteenth century that the right to resist in 1688 was a unique and never-to-be-repeated event. Locke's theories became influential, not so much in 1689, but rather with the American colonists in the 1760s and 1770s and the late eighteenth-century radicals.[10]

The debates on the transfer of the Crown reflect the very different viewpoints held by Parliamentarians and the moral dilemma which faced them. John Poley, a Tory, declared:

here is an affair of the greatest weight before us, both as we are Christians and Englishmen, no less than the deposing of a King, whom we have sworn allegiance to.... I move that this debate be adjourned till the original contract be produced and laid upon the table for the Members to peruse, that we may see whether his Majesty broke it or no.

The Prince of Orange was fourth in line in the hereditary succession to the Crown, and Tories feared placing the Crown on his head would make it elective. Sir John Chicheley, a very experienced Tory MP, thought: 'Nothing will satisfy some but placing the Crown on the Prince, which will be a precedent for placing it on another whenever the Lords and Commons please, and so consequently make this kingdom which has never been elective, into a Commonwealth, if they please, which God forbid.'[11] Another Tory MP, Gilbert Dolben, argued that James's abandonment of the government and forsaking of the kingdom amounted to a 'voluntary demise'. Sir Robert Howard, a senior Whig politician, proposed instead 'that James II had abdicated the government by breaking the original contract'. Most Tories preferred the term 'demise' to 'abdicated'. Sir George Treby bluntly pointed out: 'we have found the Crown vacant, and are to supply that defect, we found it so, we have not made it so'. Heneage Finch, Tory MP for Oxford University, who had been counsel for the Seven Bishops, opposed the idea of a vacancy: 'for us to limit the succession is plainly to say we may choose a king and is this called the prudence we ought to act with, to destroy that constitution of the government, which we come here to maintain?'[12] The voice of the 'Old Cause' was heard from Sir John Maynard, who had sat in the two Parliaments of 1640 as well as in two of Cromwell's. Lame and toothless, he rose to say:

> I am of the opinion that the King has deposed himself. All government had at first its foundation from a pact with the people, and here no one can say but this pact has apparently been broken by the King's invading and violating our laws, property, liberty, and religion by his putting Papists into all places of trust in the Government as fast as he could find Papists to fill them. . . . There is no Popish prince in Europe, but would destroy all Protestants, as in Spain, France and Hungary.[13]

Colonel Birch was of the same opinion: 'these forty years, we have been struggling against anti-Christ, popery and tyranny'.[14]

Sir Robert Howard declared: 'it is inconsistent with our religion and our laws to have a papist rule over us'. Sir Christopher Musgrave, a leading Tory from Cumberland, argued that the opinion of the lawyers as to the legality of deposing the King should be deferred to, adding that he lived near Scotland and no one knew what his neighbour would do. Thomas Wharton, on the other hand, replied: 'whether he may be deposed or depose himself, he is not our king. It is not for mine nor the interest of most here, that he should come again.'[15] Sir William Pulteney, a Whig, thought that if the Crown 'descends not from Heaven' then it must 'be from the people'.[16] Lawyers tried in vain to find precedents for unprecedented events. In the end, in a committee of the whole House, with Richard Hampden, a Presbyterian Whig, in the chair, the Commons resolved: 'that King James the Second, having endeavoured to subvert the constitution of the kingdom, by breaking the original contract, between king and people, and by the advice of the Jesuits and other wicked persons having violated the fundamental laws, and having withdrawn himself out of the kingdom, has abdicated the government, and that the throne is thereby vacant'.

In the Lords, there was a majority of peers either loyal to James, or Maryites, but they lost the initiative when Halifax, who was acting as their Speaker, moved that they delay their debate of the constitutional position until after 29 January, when the Commons would have finished consideration of the state of the nation. This motion passed despite strong opposition from Lords Nottingham, Chesterfield, Clarendon, Rochester,

Abingdon and others. On 19 January the Lords debated the Commons resolution in committee, with Danby in the chair. The Loyalists, headed by Clarendon, said in law the King 'can do no wrong', while the Bishop of Ely denounced the Commons's resolution as 'accumulative treason'. Nottingham insisted the present situation did not mean the King had forfeited the throne, much less that a Convention could depose him. The Duke of Grafton, who had taken part in the Army Plot, and the Duke of Ormonde, who had rallied to the Prince of Orange, both voted against the transfer of the Crown in all divisions. The Earl of Rochester declared that monarchy could not be elective and proposed a Regency, a motion that was lost by only three votes, 51 to 48. On 30 January, when Parliament did not sit normally as it commemorated the execution of Charles I, the Tories, supported by most bishops, argued that abdication was a voluntary act and persuaded the peers to amend the Commons vote by changing the word 'abdicated' to 'deserted', notwithstanding a strong speech by Lord Delamer, who regarded himself as absolved of any allegiance to James, which could come as no surprise to the noble lords as he had been involved in Monmouth's rebellion. On the other side, the Earl of Pembroke said quitting the kingdom 'was no more than a man's running out of his house when on fire, or a seaman throwing his goods overboard in a storm, to save his life, which could never be understood as a renunciation of his house or goods', but his argument was ignored.[17] The City of London petitioned the Lords, urging them to agree that the throne was vacant.[18] Notwithstanding, the next day, the Lords removed any reference to a vacancy, defeated a motion to declare William and Mary king and queen and carried a motion to delete the words 'and that the throne is thereby vacant' by 55 votes to 41, with the Maryites apparently joining the Loyalists.

In the Commons Sir Joseph Tredenham, a Danbyite, argued that it was 'inconsistent with the safety and welfare of the Protestant kingdom to be governed by a Popish prince', which ruled out James and his son, but he opposed the vacancy: 'The crown is always successive, never elective. Princess Mary should succeed as the next Protestant heir (and as for her being a woman, Queen Elizabeth was so and reigned gloriously).' This ruled out William and cost Tredenham his post as Vice-Warden of the Stannaries, through which he managed Cornish elections. Sir Thomas Clarges said the Crown was hereditary but that he would accept James had 'abdicated', that the throne was vacant, and that it ought to devolve to the next Protestant successor. The motion to agree with the Lords that the throne was not vacant was defeated by 282 votes to 151. The minority included Isaac Newton, the famous scientist, who presumably acted in deference to the wishes of his constituency, Cambridge University. The 151 MPs were blacklisted in a pamphlet distributed at the 1690 general election as having opposed William and Mary as king and queen. The deadlock between the two Houses was broken on 6 February when six Tory lords gave in because, as Lord Thanet told Clarendon, 'there was an absolute necessity of having a Government, and he did not see it likely to be any other way than this'.[19] The final compromise between the Houses dropped the notion of an original contract, declaring that James had abdicated and that the throne was therefore vacant.

The Prince of Orange revealed his hand at last. He would be no 'doge of Venice' (a mere figurehead), nor his wife's gentleman usher, and he let it be known publicly that he would settle for nothing less than the Crown. According to Burnet, he threatened to go back to Holland and 'meddle no more in their affairs'.[20] If true, it was bluff, for how could he go back to the Dutch States who had financed his expedition at vast cost, nor to his European allies, empty-handed? Sir John Reresby, a prominent Tory MP, wrote: 'the Prince declared that he had no design for the Crown, and yet he sought it all he could. He came to settle the Protestant religion, and yet he brought over 4000 papists in his army, which were near as many as the King had English of that religion in his.'[21] In the end, the English paid for their own invasion, reimbursing the Dutch the cost of the expedition and even making up the pay of Dutch soldiers to the level of English pay. Although the debates in Parliament on the transfer of the Crown were relatively free and untrammelled by the constitutional convention which prevented its Members from criticising the King directly, the reality was that there was a huge Dutch army in and around London, while English troops had been sent away and those who objected were powerless. Mary, who was still in Holland, conveyed through Burnet her wish to rule jointly with her husband.[22] By the Coronation Oath Act, William and Mary agreed to govern 'according to the statutes of Parliament agreed on, and the laws and customs of the same', and to maintain 'the protestant reformed religion, established by law'. This was a sop to the Tories. Nottingham agreed to chair the committee to draw up the new oath of allegiance which made subjects swear to be 'faithful and bear true allegiance to William and Mary', dropping the words 'rightful and lawful' before 'king and queen', which accommodated those like himself who would accept William as king *de facto* but not *de jure*. At William's insistence, in future the service of prayer for deliverance from the Gunpowder Plot on 5 November was amended to include thanks for the 'happy arrival' of the Prince of Orange and 'the Deliverance of our Church and Nation'.[23] John Somers, the great Whig lawyer, who became prominent at this time, proposed that William should have sole administration of the government and that the Crown should descend to William and Mary's issue, then to Mary's, then to Anne's. Mary was childless and Anne had no surviving issue, but a clause that the Crown should devolve next on Sophia, Electress of Hanover, the next Protestant heir, was omitted, presumably because Sophia was so distant in the hereditary succession. The birth of the Duke of Gloucester, Anne's son, in the summer of 1689 appeared to assure the succession. It was believed that it was Lord Churchill, who had become Anne's favourite as he had been her father's, who persuaded Anne to postpone her own claim if Mary died while William lived.[24] All this left James in the position of King Lear, faced with usurping daughters. In the end, the Commons had it both ways, the reality of an elected king and the pretence of an hereditary Crown.[25] What contemporaries would not admit to, nor historians until recently, is that it had been an invasion. Burnet, in a Pastoral Letter written as Bishop of Salisbury in 1689, claimed it had been a conquest. His aim was to make it easier for the members of the clergy, who could not accept the legality of the transfer of the Crown by Parliament, to take the oaths to William and Mary and thus avoid being ejected. This, however, was totally unacceptable to Parliament, who ordered Burnet's Letter to be burned by the common hangman in 1693.[26]

Alongside the settlement of the Crown, Parliament had been considering 'heads of grievances', which turned into the celebrated Declaration of Rights, which became a statute as the Bill of Rights [1 Wm. and Mary 2 cap. 2]. This is of special interest to American historians because of its influence on their own Declaration of Independence of 1796. Lois Schwoerer has devoted a meticulously researched monograph to the Declaration of Rights. Unlike the French Declaration of the Rights of Man in 1789 and the American Bill of Rights, the Bill of Rights of 1689, in contrast, was less concerned with the rights of individual as with the rights of Parliament. The American Declaration asserted rights for the individual which had not been secured in England in 1689. The committee drafting it was dominated by Whigs and was greatly influenced by Somers. In this matter as in others, however, Tories as well as Whigs were concerned, not to defend the royal prerogative as had been their traditional role, but to obtain as many concessions for Parliament as they could. The Declaration sought to preserve the rights of Parliament rather than the rights of the subject. It gave no specific right to individuals and no constitutional defence against the power of the King in Parliament. It left the English as mere subjects with no basic rights of their own, hence the appeals from this country to the European Court today. The Declaration looked to the past as well as to the future. It condemned the dispensing power of the King (by which James II had suspended the operation of the Test Act and Penal Laws against Roman Catholics and Protestant Dissenters) and the imprisonment of those who petitioned against it (the Seven Bishops). It condemned James's Ecclesiastical Commission and his collecting taxes before they had been granted to him by Parliament. James had maintained a standing army in time of peace without the consent of Parliament, disarmed some Protestants and armed and employed Papists, which was contrary to law. He infringed the freedom of elections and devolved to the King's Bench cases which belonged to Parliament. Corrupt and partial persons were impanelled on juries and, in cases of high treason, persons chosen who were not freeholders. Too high bails and fines had been imposed on persons accused, even before judgement was given. After condemning James's actions, the Declaration went on to define rights and duties:

> It is illegal to suspend laws by royal authority without the consent of Parliament. It is illegal to levy taxes without the consent of Parliament. It is illegal to prosecute those who petition the King. To maintain an army in time of peace without the consent of Parliament is illegal. Protestants only are entitled to bear arms. The election of Members of Parliament must be free. Freedom of speech and debates in Parliament should be subject to the jurisdiction of Parliament only. No excessive fines should be imposed. Juries should be impanelled according to the usual practice and in cases of high treason should be freeholders. All fines and forfeitures before judgment is pronounced are illegal.

Finally, in order to correct abuses, 'Parliaments should be held frequently.'[27]

The Declaration of Rights was not conditional on, but went alongside, the offer of the Crown to William and Mary. At a ceremony in the Banqueting Hall on 13 February, William and Mary accepted the Crown first and then received the Declaration. William had made public his opposition to curbing the royal prerogative, which remained intact. Clauses in the Declaration to prevent the Crown from shortening or prolonging sessions of Parliament, for religious toleration, for judges holding office during good behaviour, rather than during royal pleasure, and for regulating trials for treason, were dropped. The Prince and Princess were to hold the Crown jointly: 'the sole and full exercise of the regal power be only in and executed by the said Prince of Orange' and, in default of their issue, the Crown would devolve to Anne, Princess of Denmark and her issue. The Tories were angry at having been duped by the Prince taking the Crown and on 13 February, Sir John Reresby remarked that 'a great many looked very sadly upon it'.[28] The new oath of allegiance made people swear 'to be faithful and bear true allegiance' to the King and Queen. The new oath of supremacy detested and abjured the detestable doctrine that princes could be excommunicated or deprived by the Pope of Rome and that no foreign princes or powers were to have any jurisdiction in this realm. No king or queen in future should be in communion with the Church of Rome or marry a Papist [1 Wm & Mary caps. 3–5]. On 23 February the Convention declared itself a Parliament. The settling of the Crown and the succession and the Bill of Rights had gone through relatively quickly. The rest of that Parliament saw ferocious party squabbles and attempts to pay off old scores which paralysed much of the business and appalled William, who was unaccustomed to the ways of Parliament.

The size of the Royal Household was enlarged to its 1660 state, with its members being paid even more irregularly than in the reign of Charles II. William III showed favour to his Dutch friends Bentinck, Groom of the Stole, who became Earl of Portland, and to Zuylestein and Auverquerque. All the members of the old royalist families, who had served the Stuarts for generations, were thrown out and replaced by Whigs, some of whom were republicans.[29] Dr William Blackader, a rebel at Bothwell Brig in 1679 and one who took part in Argyll's invasion in 1685 and was twice pardoned, became the King's physician.[30] William was unsociable by nature and he thought the air in central London was bad for his asthma. He retreated to Kensington Palace and to Hampton Court, where he and Mary carried out extensive building works. After her death in 1694 and the burning down of Whitehall Palace in 1698, the Court ceased to be the social and cultural centre of English life. Charles II and James II had been keen patrons of the theatre at Whitehall, but William would not have understood English plays. It is not surprising, therefore, that much of the literature post-1689 was not celebratory of William as the 'Deliverer', but was censorial and, with Dryden in the forefront, secretly Jacobite.[31] Devonshire, one of the 'Immortal Seven', became Lord Steward, and Thomas Wharton Comptroller of the Household. Danby had expected to be made Lord Treasurer once again to reward his great service to William, but he was disappointed and had to settle for the post of Lord President of the Council. It was not Danby but Halifax, the Lord Privy Seal, who had refused to subscribe to the Invitation to the Prince of Orange in 1688, who had the new King's ear and was First Minister. William seems to have distrusted those who had plotted with him before 1688, thinking that if they had betrayed James, they would betray him too (and he was frequently right). He had nothing but contempt for Sir William Waller or William Harbord, who had sailed from Holland with him in 1688.[32] The Treasury was put in commission, composed mainly of Whigs, with the erratic Charles Mordaunt, Earl of Monmouth, as First Lord, and the ever pliant and very experienced Lord Godolphin, a moderate Tory, doing the business. William did not employ Whigs only. Often, as in the navy, Whig and Tory officers were mixed in the crews to keep an eye on one another. This was wise, and avoided driving Tories into the arms of James, though it produced sometimes chaotic government. It was essential to conciliate the Tories, many of whom were resentful still. Robert Harley, Sir Edward Harley's son, noted at this time that the clergy and many Tories 'do with all the malice imaginable express their dislike of the present government'.[33] The Whig Earl of Shrewsbury, one of the Seven, became senior Secretary of State (for the South) while the Tory Earl of Nottingham was junior Secretary (for the North).

Most annoyingly for William, Parliament refused to settle the revenue from the Customs and the Excise on him for life, as Charles II and James II had had, but for four years only. The expense of the war against France was very great and William III was not in a position to dictate to Parliament over money. The supply for the army and the navy was voted annually by Parliament. This resulted in an important constitutional change: annual sessions of Parliament. On 1 March 1689 Wharton announced that the King had agreed to give up the unpopular hearth tax. This was meant as an inducement to Parliament to grant the proceeds from another tax in lieu. Instead of granting more generous supplies, however, the Commons voted the ordinary revenue only until 24 June next.

There were other disagreements between the King and his new subjects. As a Calvinist, William had little sympathy for the Church of England and he had scoffed at the 'foolish old Popish ceremony' of the coronation.[34] The Whigs he was closest to were associated with Deists and Unitarians (those who did not believe in the Trinity). This is why, in John Kenyon's words, 'the Revolution was an abrupt reversal of every trend in Anglican thinking since 1660'.[35] William expected that Protestant

Dissenters would be given freedom of worship and access to office and was persuaded by Richard Hampden and Baron Wharton, Thomas's father, that a comprehension of the Presbyterians within the Church of England and changing Anglican ceremonial to suit them was possible. Halifax disabused him, saying that 'the Church of England had rather turn Papist than take in the Presbyterians'.[36] Devonshire, who was a strong Anglican, similarly dissuaded him. Dennis Granville, Dean of Durham, thought that the Church of England could no more be saved from Amsterdam than it could be saved from Salamanca.[37] The Toleration Act of 1689 did not give toleration to Protestant Dissenters as such, but exempted Presbyterians and those who believed in the Trinity from the penalties of the Test Acts. It did nothing for the Unitarians, the Quakers or the Jews, and left Roman Catholics more vulnerable than ever. The Revolution produced Schism in the Church of England when many bishops, including five out of the Seven, and over 400 clergy refused to take the oaths, were henceforth called the Nonjurors, and lost their livings. Those ejected sought refuge in Jacobite and High Anglican families as domestic chaplains, tutors or librarians, much as Richard Baxter and Protestant Nonconformist ministers had done after the Restoration of 1660. From 1689 there were many lay Nonjurors too, such as the Duke of Beaufort, the Earl of Exeter and Lord Chesterfield, who consequently lost their seats in Parliament. Ironically enough, this strengthened William's hold on the Lords as they were replaced by Low Church Whig bishops and as High Anglican numbers in the Lords were depleted by death or loss of their seats. The Whigs made no opposition to the suspension of the Habeas Corpus Act to enable the government to arrest and detain Jacobite suspects against whom there was insufficient legal evidence, and this became a regular feature of post-revolutionary England.

In May 1689 William got what he had come for: England declared war against France. Ever since 1672, when the Dutch cut the sluices and flooded their country to stop Louis XIV's advance, William had been obsessed with the French threat, even though Louis's campaign in the Rhineland in 1688–89 did not threaten the Dutch Netherlands. The fact is, that apart from commercial rivalry, France had presented no threat to the British Isles until Louis assisted James in the Irish wars.

Much of the time of the 1689 Parliament was spent on the case of Titus Oates, who petitioned the Lords for a writ of error to reverse the judgements against him, a procedure which turned on the legality of the original proceedings and not on the facts of the case. Oates had an unfavourable reception and Danby, now Marquess of Carmarthen, said the best way to reverse judgement was 'to whip him back to the place from whence he came'. The Commons took a different view. Sir John Maynard thought it did not matter whether what Oates had said was true or false, as 'Oates was an enemy of the Popish religion.'[38] The Commons affirmed the reality of the Popish Plot and passed a bill to reverse judgement, when the Tories present 'hissed'. This produced a deadlock between the two Houses. In the end the King pacified Oates by granting him a pension of £10 a week (which Queen Anne later discontinued) and £200 to pay his debts, where-upon he became a Baptist preacher.[39] Another paying off of scores was the 'murder committee' of the House of Lords investigating the attainders of Lord Russell, Algernon Sidney and others after the Rye House Plot. The Council of Six, who managed the Rye House Plot, had met at the house of John Hampden, Richard Hampden's son, and on 18 November 1689 Hampden told the committee 'the foundation of this glorious revolution was laid in the Council of Six whereof he had the honour to be a member'.[40] This was the first time the words 'glorious revolution' were used. Burnet also confirmed the reality of the Rye House Plot before the committee, and contradicted the evidence of Lord Russell and the 'Whig martyrs' at their trials. Thomas Wharton was so furious at this revelation that he made sure John Hampden never sat in Parliament again.[41]

The Whigs wanted to make so many exceptions to the bill of indemnity, by excepting their political opponents, as to make it useless. They tried to impeach Carmarthen (Danby), and pressed for the removal of Halifax. An Act was passed to reverse the *quo warranto* judgement against the City of London, which had thrown the Whigs out of office in the reign of Charles II, and to restore the charter of the City of London with its ancient rights and privileges [1 Wm. & Mary cap. 8]. The final straw, as far as William was concerned, however, was the 'Sacheverell clause' of January 1690. This was an amendment brought by the Whig William Sacheverell to the corporation bill to restore corporations to their pre-1675 state, and it proposed that all officials who had surrendered the charters of corporations should be ineligible for office for seven years. This would have excluded many Tories. The Whigs then threatened William that if he would not give his assent to the clause, they would not vote money bills.[42] William told Halifax that the Commons had 'used him like a dog' and that 'a King of England who will govern by law as he must do ... is the worst figure in Christendom. He has power to destroy the nation and not to protect it.'[43] The King lost patience and dissolved Parliament.

7

SCOTLAND AND THE REVOLUTION

The only country to have a common frontier with England was Scotland, an independent kingdom with its own Parliament and a legal system based on Roman law, not, as in England, common law. It had five universities as against England's two and Scots, if poorer, were generally better educated. Like Ireland, it was united to England by the Stuart kings in a personal union of the Crown. The Scottish Parliament was less developed as an institution than the English Parliament. The different estates, nobles, bishops (until 1689), Members (Barons) from each shire and one Member from each of the royal burghs all sat in one chamber, with the chief officers of the Crown. A Committee of 32, besides the officers of state, called the Lords of the Articles, prepared the legislation. There was no provision for Parliament to sit regularly, only the King could summon it and there was no obligation to do so. Lauderdale described it in 1674 as 'useless at best'.[1] The Scottish Privy Council played a more important role. The Scottish nobility, one of the most powerful in Europe, called the tune. It was dominated by the Dukes of Atholl, Argyll, Hamilton and the Marquess of Queensberry.[2]

After the Restoration, the Episcopalians, the equivalent of the Church of England, became the established Church and were the majority in 1689. They were governed by the Archbishops of St Andrews and twelve bishops, who increased the number of crown supporters in Parliament. They had preached the divine right of kings and the doctrine of nonresistance as enthusiastically as their Anglican counterparts. James, who governed Scotland in the years 1680–82 during the Exclusion Crisis in England, led an artistic renaissance with the rebuilding of much of Holyrood Palace, the commissioning of the Stuart portraits and the revival of the Order of the Thistle, which indicated a revival of crown interest in Scotland. This was popular with the aristocracy, who flocked to the Court at Edinburgh. James II and VII of Scotland enjoyed a more secure position in Scotland than his brother Charles had. The Duke of Argyll, who had fled the kingdom in 1681 (like Shaftesbury in England), led a rebellion in Scotland in 1685, but he had lost much of his power-base while he was in exile and he received little aristocratic support. The government acted speedily by arresting suspects, crushing the rebels and executing Argyll on the basis of a previous conviction for high treason. The atmosphere changed in 1685, however, when the normally docile Parliament, when offered free trade with England in return, refused to grant toleration to Roman Catholics. As a result, James dismissed Parliament in 1687.[3] The Duke of Perth, the Lord Chancellor, and his brother the Earl of Melfort, both converts to Roman Catholicism, were James's chief advisers in Scotland and later in exile at Saint-Germain-en-Laye. Despite their dislike of Presbyterianism, they implemented James's policy of toleration for Presbyterians in 1687 and they duly presented an address of thanks. Sir John Dalrymple, the Lord Advocate (son of Sir James Dalrymple, Lord Stair, a Presbyterian), collaborated enthusiastically with James. As in England, the numbers of the Catholic minority are difficult to estimate. The leading Catholic peer, the Duke of Gordon, became Governor of Edinburgh in 1685 and was later given a place on the Council and the Treasury, but he was less influential.[4]

The Scots had taken no part in the Invitation or secret negotiations with William of Orange before 1688, and the Scottish nobility did nothing at the time of the Dutch invasion. The Scots seemed little concerned until Lord Chancellor Perth's flight on 10 December 1688 and James's final departure on 23 December.[5] A Convention was summoned, which met on 14 March 1689. Jacobites were almost as numerous there as opponents of James. The Episcopalians had disliked James's policy of toleration, but they had been loath to oppose him and they were and remained the mainstay of Jacobitism. There was a contest over the presidency of the assembly between William Douglas, 3rd Duke of Hamilton and John Murray, 2nd Duke of Atholl, representing the Jacobites. James's letter to the Convention demanding unconditional obedience disheartened his supporters and Atholl left.[6]

The lead was then taken by 'the Club', a sophisticated opposition group, which seized the initiative from Hamilton and acted in opposition to Sir John Dalrymple, James's turncoat Lord Advocate. Sir James Montgomerie of Skermorlie was the central figure, with the support of his kinsman Archibald Campbell, 10th Earl of Argyll.[7] They sought a Presbyterian settlement for the Church and supremacy of Parliament in the constitution. On 4 April the Convention voted that James had not abdicated, but 'by doing acts contrary to law' had forfeited his right to the Crown.[8] A Claim of Right, passed on 11 April, laid down that James had invaded the fundamental constitution of the kingdom and altered it from a legal, limited monarchy to an arbitrary despotic power. It condemned prelacy as 'a great and insupportable grievance'. Two days later, the Act of Grievances called for the repeal of the Act of Supremacy of 1669 and the abolition of the Lords of the Articles. Sir John Dalrymple wrote that the redressing of all grievances was to be a condition of the offer of the Crown of Scotland. Would William accept such curbs on the royal prerogative? The commissioners sent to London to offer the Crown to William and Mary on 11 May were Argyll, Montgomerie and Sir John Dalrymple. It was meant to be conditional on the Claim of Right and the Articles of Grievances being accepted by William first, but Dalrymple altered the order in which the documents were read in order to remove the implication that the offer of the Crown was conditional. Meanwhile John Graham of Claverhouse, Viscount Dundee, who had commanded the King's army at Bothwell Brigg, raised the Stuart standard, and although he failed to attract widespread support from the Episcopalians and the North-East Lowlands, he defeated the Williamite forces at Killiecrankie on 27 July 1689, but he was killed at the battle, which proved a pyrrhic victory. The Duke of Gordon, who had been holding Edinburgh Castle for James, surrendered. Sir James Montgomerie had wanted to be Secretary of State for Scotland and was angry when Lord Melville, who had been in exile in the United Provinces, was appointed instead. In a quick volte-face, Montgomerie became a Jacobite working for James's restoration on constitutional terms and urging the Episcopalians to take the oaths in order to serve James in the Scottish Parliament. He teamed up with Robert Ferguson (who had come over from the Netherlands as William's Presbyterian chaplain and then became a Jacobite when he thought the Prince had betrayed his promises), to urge Whig Dissenters in the English Parliament not to vote William any money.[9] Montgomerie died in exile at Saint-Germain-en-Laye, after James had made him his Secretary of State for Scotland and granted him a pension.

The Scottish Parliament abolished the Lords of the Articles, abolished the royal supremacy over the Church and won some measure of independence from crown control. The King did not lose all political management, as he kept the appointment of the officers of state and, above all, of the Privy Councillors, who exercised considerable legislative, judicial and executive powers. Patronage and venality helped the Crown, but the magnates kept the whip hand.[10] The Whig exiles had repeatedly misinformed William by saying that the Presbyterians were three-quarters of the people of Scotland. William's appointment of George, Lord Melville, who had taken part in the Monmouth rebellion and fled to Holland in 1685, served to strengthen this outlook.[11] The major part of the nobility were 'not for Presbytery'. Nevertheless, William might have considered a moderate episcopal system, had not the bishops and the Episcopalians continued their allegiance to James. The result was the abolition of official prelacy. This produced a schism in the Church, as James and his successors continued to name Episcopalian bishops. The Presbyterians were vindictive towards the Episcopalians, abolishing private patrons, and turning 664 clergymen out of their livings, even those who had conformed. In addition they purged the universities and seized the cathedrals.[12] The General Assembly of the Church of Scotland secured a quasi-parliamentary role when the separation of Church and State was recognised.[13] William continued this Parliament for the rest of his reign, without ever holding an election. The reign of William III left unhappy memories in Scotland. The Highland War, which continued until 1692 (then and later the Clan chiefs were paid off to remain quiet), the massacre of the Macdonalds at Glencoe in 1692 (which was approved by William), the famines of 1697 and 1699, and the failure of the Darien Company, Scotland's only colonial venture in 1699–1700, with great loss of lives and money in the face of opposition from England and Spain, rankled in popular memory. William was indifferent to Scotland and never went there. This period of Scottish history is known as 'King William's seven ill years'.[14]

The Revolution settlement in Scotland had not provided for a union of the Crowns of England and Scotland in future or to prevent the Scots from recalling their Stuart King. In 1702, soon after Queen Anne's accession, commissioners were appointed to treat for a union with Scotland to provide for the Crown passing to the House of Hanover on the death of Queen Anne, but this was unpopular with Tory MPs, who thought Scotland would be a liability, as Scotland was poorer than England.[15] In 1704 the Scottish Parliament passed the Act of Security, which stated that it had a right to nominate a sovereign of the royal family of Scotland who *must not* be the successor to the English throne. The motivation was loyalty to the Stuarts for some, and for others it was a ploy to win commercial concessions from England. It further passed an Act allowing for the import of French wines and the export of wool to France, which were banned in England, but could easily be brought into England from Scotland. The English Parliament retaliated with the Alien Act, which provided that if the Act of Security were not repealed, either by an Act of Union or by accepting the Hanoverian succession, the Scots would be treated as aliens in England, and their principal exports to England – linen, cattle and coal – prohibited. In the 1705 Westminster Parliament, Lord Treasurer Godolphin had a majority for an incorporating union, which for the Scots seemed like the end of their independence, spanning over 1000 years of history. Robert Harley, who managed the Commons for Godolphin, financed a propaganda campaign in Scotland in favour of the Union, with the assistance of Daniel Defoe and Thomas Patterson, a Scottish economist who had suggested the foundation of the Bank of England. Defoe reported that the Scots were 'ripe for every mischief' and that 'the very Whigs declare openly they will join with France and King James or any body rather than be insulted by the English'.[16]

The campaign against the Union was led by George Lockhart of Carnwarth, a prominent member of the Scottish Parliament and a Jacobite, and by Fletcher of Saltoun, a much respected republican Whig and a Monmouth rebel, who argued that the Revolution Settlement in Scotland had corrected none of the abuses and high-handedness complained of in the reign of James II and VII. Fletcher thought that the Westminster system of the Crown in Parliament gave it absolute powers, unchecked by anyone. Many Presbyterians opposed the Union for reasons of patriotism, though most were brought round as it made the Kirk, the established Church, independent from England. The great territorial magnates dominated Scottish politics. The Duke of Hamilton, who opposed the Union, was ineffective. The Marquess of Queensberry, a Whig who led the *squadrone volante*, an unprincipled group of politicians who followed only their self-interest, led the support for the Union, after receiving a £20 000 bribe from England. As Patrick Riley revealed, the Union was brought about by bribery and intimidation on a massive scale. £100 000, called the Equivalent, was paid to Scotland as compensation for assuming a share of the English national debt and to encourage Scottish industries. Commissioners were appointed to treat for the Union, which was to begin on 1 May 1707. The government would not risk holding an election in Scotland, so that Scottish MPs were co-opted to the Parliament at Westminster. The Scottish nobility, which was as numerous as its English counterpart, was represented at Westminster by 16 Representative peers only. In the Commons Scotland had 45 MPs, only one more than

Cornwall, with single-Member constituencies, with 30 seats for the counties and 15 for the burghs, which chose Members in rotation. Scotland and Cornwall played a crucial part in eighteenth-century politics by ensuring the government of the day almost always had a majority in Parliament. The Scottish electorate was small and easily manipulated. The Scottish MPs were paid £10 a week to attend and proved pliable. The name of Scotland was abolished and Scots were to be known henceforth as North Britons. The English, however, were in no hurry to call themselves South Britons! There was resentment at the abolition of the Scottish Privy Council, which had been an influential instrument of government. Scotland did retain its separate judicial system, based on Roman law, not common law, and its educational system.[17] The Scots, however, resented the higher taxes imposed after the Union.

The 1708 attempt to restore the Stuarts, with the help of a substantial French expedition, met with widespread support in Scotland, where national pride had been deeply wounded by the circumstances of the Union. In England, the Jacobites showed little inclination to co-operate with their Scottish counterparts, but were content to wait until the eventual death of Queen Anne. The expedition, led by James III, would probably have landed successfully. It miscarried largely through treachery. The recently discovered logbook of a French ship has revealed that the French naval officer directing navigation (he was presumably in the pay of England) deliberately sailed by the Firth of Forth, the place agreed with the Jacobites for the landing.[18] Thus a good opportunity to restore the Stuarts and repeal the Union was wasted.

The greatest long-term advantage of the Union was that the Scots, unlike the Irish, were given access to the English domestic and colonial markets. This made little impact at first as 90 per cent of the population lived off the land, but long-term it was of great economic benefit to Scotland. The 1715 and 1745 Jacobite rebellions were supported overwhelmingly by the Episcopalians, Roman Catholics and many Presbyterians, driven by the desire to break the incorporating Union as well as to restore the Stuarts, Scotland's ancient kings. They resulted, in 1716 and 1746, in a mass population exodus to France, Russia, Sweden and Prussia.[19] They became soldiers, seamen, merchants, bankers and physicians. They founded the Russian navy under Peter the Great and helped to train the armies of Frederick the Great of Prussia. Those who were transported or emigrated to North America made a major contribution to the life of that continent as well. An early Jacobite exile of a different type was John Law, the Scottish economist, who went to James II's court at

St-Germain, and became chief minister of France in 1720, when he attempted unsuccessfully to bring the financial revolution to France.[20] Those who left the country were Britain's loss and continental Europe's and America's gain.

8

IRELAND AND THE REVOLUTION

Scotland was an independent kingdom, but Ireland was a dependent kingdom under the Crown. Deep in the Irish Protestant psyche was the memory of the massacre of Protestants by Irish Catholics in 1641. But deep in the Catholic psyche was the memory of the slaughter of Irish Catholics like beasts in the field by Cromwell's troops at Drogheda in 1649 and the confiscation of their lands, which were given to Protestant settlers, mainly Scottish Presbyterians. At the Restoration, as in England, Charles II did not attempt to reverse the land settlement. Charles provided more relaxed rules for the Catholic majority, who could own land and practise professions. Catholics and Ulster Presbyterians were excluded from office under the Crown by the provisions of the Test Act of 1673. The Irish Parliament, in which Catholics sat at this time, was subordinate to the English Parliament, as Poynings Law provided that laws passed by the Irish Parliament had to be approved by the Westminster Parliament first. However, Charles II did not call the Irish Parliament after 1666 and used money from Customs due to meet the shortfall of his English revenue. The Lord-Lieutenant or Vice-Roy exercised royal power in the King's name and the 1st Duke of Ormonde, the greatest of all Lord-Lieutenants, managed to keep Ireland quiet when the so-called Popish Plot was exported to Ireland and Oliver Plunkett, Archbishop of Armagh, and other Catholics were executed. The Boyles, Earls of Burlington and Irish Anglican magnates, were hereditary Lord Treasurers of Ireland, but the post was not influential.[1] The important posts of Vice-Treasurer and others were given for reasons of English politics, not for Irish considerations. The Church of Ireland, the equivalent of the Church of England but in a small minority instead of the majority as in England, had a monopoly of office. Ormonde's successor in 1685, the

Earl of Clarendon, brother-in-law of the Earl of Rochester, the very able and financially honest Lord Treasurer of England, continued Anglican hegemony even after the accession of James II, a Catholic king.[2] Clarendon was succeeded in 1687 by Richard Talbot, Earl of Tyrconnel, an Irish Catholic. With characteristic partiality, in order to discredit Tyrconnel and his measures to give political power to the Catholic majority in Ireland, Macaulay described Tyrconnel's ancestry as 'one of those degenerate families of the Pale which were popularly classed with the aboriginal population of Ireland'.[3] With Tyrconnel, the Catholic majority ceased to be invisible. He secured the appointment of Catholic Sheriffs and the surrender of charters. Between 1687 and 1688 Catholics were granted freedom of worship and the right to hold office, so that by November 1688 they controlled the administration in Dublin, the Irish judiciary, the army, the militia, the commissions of the peace and the borough corporations. James repeatedly insisted on fair treatment for his Irish Protestant subjects and that no one should be deprived of office on grounds of religion, but he had far less co-operation from Protestant Dissenters, except for the Quakers, than in England. Some Irish Catholics urged Tyrconnel to break the land settlement and free Irish trade from the restrictions imposed on England.[4] When James landed in Ireland in March 1689, making a triumphal entry into Dublin on 3 April, he relied, as he admitted, mainly on his Catholic subjects.[5] They were full of zeal, but they were not professional soldiers, and lacked training, as well as arms and equipment in sufficient quantities. Louis XIV, who had no territorial designs in Ireland, provided him at first with officers only. When he sent troops, he denied James the Irish troops in French service, who would have put their hearts and soul into the struggle, sending instead mercenaries captured by the French, ironically enough mostly Protestants like the Danes (Lutherans), who were not dedicated to Louis's or James's service. The Scottish Jacobites, who had risen under Viscount Dundee, begged James to send forces from Ireland to assist them, and James was inclined to send troops from Ireland into Scotland and eventually England, but the French envoy, d'Avaux, advised against it, arguing the whole of Ireland must be secured first.[6]

James had proved an able well-trained commander in the past, but he was indecisive during the Irish campaign. His Irish Parliament, which met in May 1689, summoned to raise money, was dominated by Irish Catholics and was the only representative Parliament Ireland had before independence. At that stage, it has been said, the internal and mystical government of Ireland became its external and apparent government. It pressed for the reversal of the Irish land settlement which was regarded as a symbol of oppression, and for the restoration of the Catholic Church in Ireland.[7] The House of Lords also had a Catholic majority. James, who sought to protect Irish Protestants from Catholic fellow-countrymen and French troops,[8] insisted the Church of Ireland (the Irish counterpart of the Church of England) bishops and peers should take their seats, but only four bishops and six Protestant peers attended. In the end, James had to accede to repeal the land settlement, which alarmed his High Anglican supporters in England. James, however, resisted the repeal of Poynings Law, thus keeping control at Westminster. He also refused trade concessions to France. As d'Avaux wrote: 'he has a heart too English to take any step that could vex the English'. Unfortunately full accounts of its proceedings are missing, as in 1695 the Irish Protestants had the records of this Parliament obliterated. Nevertheless, it passed 35 statutes, including one for liberty of conscience. To counter this, volunteer associations of Irish Protestants began to form in Ulster and North Connaught.[9] William King, Chancellor of St Patrick's Cathedral in Dublin, provided the backbone of resistance to James.[10] The Irish Protestants who had fled to England or joined the northern associations were outlawed. The Ulster Protestants then appealed to William III to come to their assistance, while Protestant landowners who lived isolated among Catholics tried to keep a low profile.[11] A minority of Protestants, Nonjuring clergy of the Church of Ireland, office-holders and squires in the Cavalier tradition, actively supported the Jacobite cause. Charles Leslie, a member of the Church of Ireland and one of the ablest writers of his time, became a Nonjuror and embraced Jacobitism. George Berkeley, the famous philosopher, and other clergymen of the Church of Ireland, for their part, came to regard 'Presbyterianism as a more deadly enemy than Romanism'.[12]

In August 1689 William sent 20 regiments, the best in his army, including Dutch, Danes and Huguenots, to relieve the inactive Marshal Schomberg and assist the Ulster volunteers. The latter had suffered great hardships at the siege of Londonderry, when the Apprentice Boys shut the gates against James's army. Not that William, who thought fighting was best left to professional soldiers, was grateful. He came in person, regarding going to Ireland as a 'terrible mortification', and landed near Belfast in June 1690, with 15 000 more troops and artillery, greatly out-numbering James's army. John, Baron Churchill fought with distinction on William's side. Another great general, Churchill's nephew, the Duke of Berwick, James's natural son by Arabella Churchill, John's sister, fought in James's army. At the Battle of the Boyne on 1/12 July 1690 William showed himself to be a better general than he was subsequently to prove in Flanders, defeating the Jacobite army and opening the way to Dublin and south-east Ireland.[13] Part of James's army retreated westwards beyond the Shannon towards Limerick with Patrick Sarsfield, Catholic Ireland's hero, while James himself and most of his troops withdrew to France.[14] In this situation, the Catholic Irish were divided into the peace party, ready to accept whatever terms the Williamites might offer, and the war party, hoping that Sarsfield successes might lead the French to send more help or that William might be defeated on the continent of Europe. The Battle of Aughrim in County Galway on 12 July 1691, at which Tyrconnel and St Ruth, the French generals were both killed, was a close-run thing. The population suffered from the lawless violence of Catholic rapparees and from Williamite and Jacobite army deserters. The terms of the Treaty of Limerick tried to conciliate Catholics by preserving the lands of the Catholics who surrendered, probably to avoid trouble and to encourage economic development. Irish Protestant colonists, who had a siege mentality, had not been consulted and concessions were gradually whittled away by the all-Protestant Irish Parliament. The Irish Parliament called in 1692, in which the Catholic majority was unrepresented, proved unmanageable and did not grant any money. On the other hand, the financial corruption of Lord Coningsby, the Paymaster-General in Ireland, and Sir Charles Porter, the Lord Chancellor, sparked off a violent row in the Westminster Parliament.

The 1695 and 1697 Irish Parliaments passed legislation which constituted a systematic code against Catholicism. In 1695–96 Lord Capel, the Lord-Lieutenant, who sympathised with the Irish Protestants, devised a new scheme to restore the Irish Treasury to solvency and pay the large standing army stationed in Ireland. A group of men known as 'Undertakers' undertook to raise the supply in return for pensions, the distribution of patronage and being given a voice in government policy. Those who governed Ireland represented about 6 per cent of its population. They finally destroyed the civil rights supposedly granted to Catholics under the terms of the Treaty of Limerick. The Ulster Presbyterians were far from being the chief beneficiaries of the Battle of the Boyne, for they continued to be excluded from the Irish Parliament and from office under the Crown.[15] French Huguenot settlers, who were Calvinists, were unwelcome in Ireland. The historical mythology centred round the deification of William of Orange by the Ulster Presbyterians, and the ceremonies of the Orange Orders did not begin until the 1790s.[16] They were a response to the French Revolution and to the United Irishmen, an influential group of Protestants and Catholics, who wanted Irish independence and appealed to France for military assistance. The Church of Ireland viewed Presbyterians with suspicion and some preferred Romanism to Presbyterianism, while some clergy became Jacobites. In 1695 bills were passed to prohibit the sending of Catholic children to be educated abroad, to disarm Catholics, and to banish Catholic bishops and regular clergy. Like the Huguenots (Protestants) in France, some Catholics kept their land by the eldest son 'converting' to the Established Church.[17] Catholics could no longer practise in the professions, sit in the Irish House of Commons or in the Lords and, after 1727, could no longer vote in elections. Irish forfeitures left Catholics with 14 per cent of the land, falling to 5 per cent as the century progressed. They had to work the land for Protestant landlords, many of them absentees, subjected to laws less designed to convert them to the Church of Ireland as to keep them permanently as social inferiors; in other words, its rulers were more anxious 'to convert Irish land than convert the Irish people'. In 1699 the English Parliament passed an act to restrict the import of Irish woollens. It was economic restrictions, the exclusion of Irish goods from the colonial as well as the English markets, which led William Molyneux to assert a Protestant Irish national consciousness. *The Case of Ireland being Bound* (1698) is a landmark in Anglo-Irish thought. It denounced the blatant subordination of Ireland and Irish self-interest to England and asserted a Protestant Irish identity. The Declaratory Act of 1720, however, which defined the legislative and jurisdictional supremacy of the British over the Irish Parliament, completed the transition of Ireland 'from kingdom to colony'.[18]

Historians of Ireland have tended to look almost exclusively to the Irish Protestants, assuming that the Catholic majority was content to lick its wounds and lie low – 'the dogs that did not bark in the night' has been one phrase used – with no real commitment to Jacobitism. There was hope and escape for Irish Catholics, however. Looking at the Stuart papers, a rich source for Ireland, at material on the continent of Europe and at sources in Irish (as Professor Ó Buchella has shown), a different picture emerges. The Irish Catholic majority longed for the return of the Stuarts as they would for the Messiah, and did not give up hope that the French or some other power would come to their relief.[19] Since 1630 there had been some Irish troops in French service, but after 1691–92 there was a flood of Irish Catholics towards the Continent. Of these, 19 000 joined the troops in James's army in France, the first of the 'Wild

Geese'. Of the confiscated Irish lands, 72 per cent belonged to these exiles.[20]

Three Irish regiments were commissioned directly by Louis XIV and 14 regiments were commissioned by James II. James had his own army until 1697. Recruitment on this scale involved close links between the exiles and Ireland itself. There was also massive flight of capital out of Ireland after 1690 and Sir Daniel Arthur, the head of a powerful network of Irish bankers, to which Richard Cantillon also belonged, held half the money of Ireland in his hands after 1689. This network and others were used to transfer funds to the Jacobite exiles under complicated financial arrangements similar to those used by the French Huguenots. There were about 40 000 Jacobite exiles in France alone between 1688 and 1692. Of these, 60 per cent were Irish, 35 per cent English and only 5 per cent Scottish until the mass emigration of the Scots after the Fifteen. Those who were Catholics found financial as well as moral support from the religious orders on the Continent, especially at the Irish College in Paris, where the Irish Catholic clergy were trained. The Jacobite exiles in France, who have been studied by Nathalie Genet-Rouffiac, had higher social standing than the Huguenots in England, were more numerous, and made an even greater contribution to France, the host country, than the Huguenots. Some exiles had a difficult time at first; others had very successful careers. General Arthur Dillon, Viscount Dillon, who went over to France, had some of the largest forfeited estates in Ireland (2800 acres in Mayo, 825 in Roscommon and 1042 in Westmeath), became Lieutenant-General in the French army, had a brilliant military career and served as James III's ambassador to the court of Versailles. His eldest son succeeded him in command of his regiment, while another became Archbishop of Toulouse and of Narbonne, so that his family entered the upper reaches of the French aristocracy. There are other examples, such as Lord Clare and General Lally.[21]

When James's army was disbanded after the Peace of Ryswick in 1697, the Irish regiments went into French pay, while many went into Spanish service. The Irish were welcomed in Spain and were given the same rights as Spanish nationals without having to be naturalised. The Irish troops in the Spanish service formed the personal guard of Philip V, Louis XIV's second grandson, and enjoyed a privileged position when the 2nd Duke of Ormonde, a Jacobite exile, was Captain-General of all the armies of Spain from 1719 to 1736. The Irish regiments were recruited in James III's name, took the oaths to him and did not regard themselves as mercenaries.[22] Others besides those in the army made the most of their opportunities. There was a network of Irish Jacobite merchants stretching from the Baltic to Malaga in Spain.[23] There was a large Jacobite Irish colony in Bilbao in northern Spain, a port from which most of the trade between Ireland and Spain flowed.[24]

The English Parliament had meant the money from the sale of Irish forfeitures to be used to pay the cost of the Irish war, but William gave away vast estates, including James's estates granted to him out of the lands of the Regicides (the men who signed Charles I's death warrant), to his favourites, particularly to the Dutch William Bentinck, Earl of Portland, to his own mistress, Elizabeth Villiers, and others. This was done without the consent of Parliament. By the Resumption Act of 1699, these grants and sales of Irish forfeitures were declared illegal by the Westminster Parliament, but the estates were not restored to their original owners unless they were Protestants, in which cases they were sold.

9

THE WAR WITH FRANCE, JACOBITE OPPOSITION, PARLIAMENT AND THE FINANCIAL SETTLEMENT

Anxious to obtain a settlement of the revenue and to get funds for the war against France, William listened to the offers of Danby, now Marquess of Carmarthen, who replaced Halifax as Chief Minister, though he could not get his heart's wish by becoming Lord Treasurer once again. Clarendon noted that the King 'had declared himself for the Church of England, and had given public encouragement...to choose Church of England men'. In disgust, Halifax turned to opposition at its most factious, opposing the Recognition Bill, which legalised the Revolution Settlement as sketched by the Convention of 1689. The general election of 1690, conducted along traditional lines with the writs being sent to the Sheriffs, produced a Tory majority. The City of London, formerly a Whig stronghold, returned four Church of England men. William III was anxious to lessen party conflicts and his speech to the new Parliament reflected this: 'I have endeavoured to extinguish (or at least compose) all differences among my subjects.' This was a vain hope, however. Most Tories would not accept William as king *de jure* but only *de facto*. This left the Tories open to Whig accusations of being disaffected. To counter this, Nottingham (himself a *de facto* Tory) warned Bentinck, Earl of Portland that the Whigs were not monarchists by principle: 'that though the Whigs caused the Prince of Orange to be crowned King, yet other people must keep him on the throne, for the principles, who set him up, would pull him down'. Wharton, on the other hand, argued that it was the Tories who were unreliable supporters of William III: 'your chief men that manage matters are such as submit to this King upon wrong principles, because he has the governing power, but will be as ready to join another when he prevails'. Wharton sought to drive the Tories out of office by introducing, unsuccessfully, bills to force them to abjure the late King James and the 'pretended Prince of Wales'. This device, according to a prominent Tory, William Bromley of Bagington in Warwickshire, was 'a snare to catch good conscientious men but will not hold the bad'.[1]

Many High Anglican Tories, however, the group who had persuaded James to restore the position of the Church of England in September 1688, would not accept William as king at all and made strenuous efforts to restore James from 1689 to 1696. These included the Duke of Beaufort, the Earls of Clarendon, Chesterfield, Lichfield, Ailesbury, Yarmouth, Weymouth, Lord Preston (who had managed the 1685 Parliament for James), the Bishop of Ely, Sir John Fenwick and other experienced army officers who had been MPs. Most but not all were Nonjurors.[2] Their allies in a brilliant anti-Williamite propaganda campaign were Whig Jacobites, such as Charlwood Lawton, Robert Ferguson, Sir James Montgomerie and Henry Care, an Exclusionist, who became a Catholic convert in James's reign and stayed faithful to him.

Notwithstanding, William, as Burnet noted, was reluctant to place himself in the hands of one party only, and preferred a system of mixed ministries, in which the balance of power tilted at times towards Tories or Whigs.[3] Multi-party ministries were an unstable system, but one which enabled Whig and Tory ministers to keep a watch on one another and one which did not drive the Tories into the wilderness, as in 1715. Shrewsbury, one of the Whigs who had issued the Invitation in 1688, was one of the Secretaries of State, while Nottingham, a Tory who had supported a Regency in 1689, though he served William III faithfully as King, was the other Secretary of State.[4] Carmarthen could not unite the Tories and the enmity between him and Sir Edward Seymour and Rochester, dating back from Charles II's reign, persisted. Most Tories were disinclined to grant William the revenue for life.

Assisted by Sir Henry Goodricke and Sir John Lowther of Lowther as his managers and the highly corrupt and pliable Sir John Trevor as Speaker, Carmarthen manipulated political patronage by rewarding court supporters in Parliament with jobs, money or other favours. This was done on a far greater scale than he had been able to do in the reign of Charles II, so that the 1690 Parliament was known as the 'Officers'' or 'office-holders'' Parliament. This Parliament contained the largest number of placemen and pensioners than any examined in this study (it could be favours for relatives too). Those most keenly sought after were places on the Boards of the Treasury, Admiralty or Trade, which were worth about £1000 a year. Very powerful connections only could secure a tellership of the Exchequer, worth about £10 000 a year. Placemen's numbers were swelled by army and naval officers and government contractors sitting in this Parliament and by the disposal of places on local commissions of the peace and militia, a source of status and electoral advantage in the country.[5] They were whipped in under threat of losing their posts or pensions. The Commons granted the Customs and Excise duties for four years only, while the supply for the army and navy were voted annually, which ensured regular sessions of Parliament. In this sense, sovereignty now lay in the King in Parliament, unrestrained by any power on earth. The royal prerogative was intact in other respects. The government of the day did not initiate major legislation as a rule, being expected to raise the supply for the army, navy and the Civil List, from which the cost of the Royal Households and secret service money for intelligence and bribes to Parliamentarians came. It was essential for the ministers to secure the choice of a favourable Chairman of the Committee of Supply, which initiated grants of money. Legislation came about as a result of petitions which were referred to committees. The committees drew up the bills, which became statutes. They consisted mainly of prominent Parliamentarians, lawyers, government officials in the case of money bills, and Members from the county where local bills were concerned.

Parliament consisted of 513 MPs and about 130 hereditary peers, 24 bishops and 2 archbishops (Canterbury and York) in the House of Lords. Most constituencies returned two members, London, Weymouth and Melcombe Regis four, and Welsh constituencies one. The unreformed House of Commons was returned on a motley electoral system evolved over centuries on a franchise of freeholders, freemen by election (that is, chosen by a corporation) or by birth and servitude (by belonging to a particular trade or guild), members of corporations, and inhabitant householders not receiving alms. More extraordinary still were the scot and lot voters, who paid certain taxes and could be manipulated by altering the tax roll, or the burgage voters, where the right of election was attached to a house or a piece of land and whose numbers could be increased by splitting burgages. Among the most esoteric constituencies were Old Sarum, a borough inhabited mainly by sheep, controlled by Governor Pitt, a wealthy East Indian (grandfather of William Pitt, Earl of Chatham); Dunwich, which was mostly submerged by the sea; or Droitwich, where the proprietors of the salt springs had the vote. Leicester, on the other hand, had universal male suffrage. The counties and the largest constituencies, such as London and Westminster, were regarded as representing the voice of public opinion and had to be taken notice of by governments. In the counties the 40-shilling (the minimum amount of tax payable) free-holders had the vote and were usually free from government or other pressure. Leaseholders for life, however, who were treated as freehold-ers, could be influenced by their landowners. Similarly, because govern-ment departments, the law courts, Parliament and the Court were in London and Westminster, they exerted a significant influence on some sections of voters. It is not generally realised that the House of Commons could alter the franchise of any borough at any time by a majority vote on the right of election. Whole areas of counties could be disenfranchised, by omitting certain regions from the electoral roll, to suit the government of the day. It was an inverse system of proportional representation. Governments habitually increased their majorities by unseating their opponents on election petitions, so that the post of Chairman of the Elections Committee was crucial. Yet apart from disenfranchising a few rotten boroughs, whose venality could no longer be tolerated, there was no general demand for parliamentary reform. Triennial Parliaments kept the country in a permanent state of electioneering, the electorate was growing, and it has been argued that parties 'created their electorates in these years'. The most dedicated party activists on behalf of the Tories were the Anglican clergy. They could not sit as MPs, as they were repre-sented in Convocation, but they could vote in parliamentary elections and organise support at elections. Roman Catholics voted at elections (unless they were tendered the oaths at the poll, which was rare), and they voted Tory, as the poll books show, though they could not sit in Parliament or hold office at national or local level. The Dissenters were the most ener-getic electoral managers for the Whigs. Computer analyses of poll books, giving the names of voters (which had to be kept after 1695), have shown that votes were cast overwhelmingly on party lines.[6] These surveys, how-ever, cannot be wholly systematic as not all poll books have survived and the identification of each voter is difficult.

Parliament, with notable exceptions, was not an altruistic body and great vested interests were well represented in it. Yet the country at large benefited also by being able to bring grievances or requests by way of petitions. Charters for the great joint-stock (with share capital held in common) companies, such as the East India, Hamburg or the Royal African Companies, had to be petitioned for to Parliament. The rivalry from 1689 between the Old, Tory-backed, East India Company and the

New, Whig-backed, East India Company resulted in Parliamentary disputes until they were merged in 1701. The building of roads, canals and ports, making rivers navigable or building workhouses, all came by way of petitions presented by MPs and bills being passed in response to them. These petitions, backed by legal counsel and witnesses, often resulted in Acts of Parliament. Petitions lapsed after one session and had to be renewed at great financial cost, so that Parliament being in session for much of the year benefited petitioners. Constituencies looked to their MPs for patronage and favours of various kinds. The great houses of aristocrats and squires provided employment for country neighbourhoods and trade for local shopkeepers, so that there was always an element of deference at the polls in the smaller boroughs, especially as there was no secret ballot. Areas of the country and large towns, such as Birmingham, Manchester and Sheffield, not represented in Parliament, could sometimes get the county Member (knight of the shire), or a Member for an adjoining constituency, to present petitions on their behalf, though they lacked the power of persuasion constituencies had. To speak of virtual representation, however, is a gross exaggeration.[7]

The Revolution of 1689 was not a populist or a radical revolution. Yet it brought massive changes in society in one respect at least: the war against France, which transformed finances and eventually turned Britain into a world power. Tudor (1585–1603) military ventures into continental Europe had been on a small scale. Cromwellian expansion in 1657–59 was modest, and it depended on a secret defensive and offensive alliance with Cardinal Mazarin's France.[8] Charles II's interventions on the Continent had been limited and brief. In contrast, Britain became involved as a major participant in massive military operations on the continent of Europe for 20 years (1689–97 and 1702–13). Britain was not used to such wars and the cultural shock was dramatic. Charles II's army, when it was disbanded in 1680, comprised 7000–8000 men; William's army in Flanders stood at 90 000–100 000 troops, mostly Dutch and British. William III sent two-thirds of the English army to the Low Countries, as he did not trust British regiments, leaving more Dutch troops than English in England. The cost of the army, excluding the navy, in which William was not very interested, was £2 700 000 a year.[9] Officers purchased their commissions, and the only qualification required was to be able to ride a horse. Most English officers, apart from those who had served in the French army under Turenne or in the Dutch forces, were less experienced in continental warfare and had to learn the hard way. A cause of great resentment for British officers in Flanders was that they were made subordinate to Dutch and German commanders. The cost of bringing recruits overseas was borne by the officers, with no obligation to bring them back, and those left stranded, if they managed to get back, often had to beg their bread in the streets. There were large-scale desertions of soldiers from William's army in Flanders to James's in France, and they were incorporated into the *Royal Etranger*, a regiment commanded by the Duke of Berwick.[10] Desertion was common at the time, but why should British soldiers desert to James's army rather than to those of wealthier princes, if not for reasons of personal allegiance? Eventually, in the War of the Spanish Succession (1702–13), pressing (forcible recruitment) for the army was introduced. In leading the army in person in Flanders, William probably tried to emulate Louis XIV, with whom he was obsessed, and who regarded commanding the army in person as the core of the *métier du roi*. Unfortunately William was not a gifted general and the first five years of his reign saw a succession of military defeats. After his very successful propaganda campaign, masterminded by Burnet in 1688, William did not bother to conceal his dislike of and contempt for his British subjects, spurning Churchill, the most gifted English commander and one who had deserted to him in 1688 and had rendered great services in the Irish wars. William probably thought Churchill would betray him as he had betrayed James. There was some justification for this belief, as Churchill had in fact been engaged in serious Jacobite dealings with James in the 1690s and was sent to the Tower on charges of high treason.[11] Churchill was politically important as he and his wife Sarah (herself a Whig) presided at a rival court, that of Princess Anne, James's second daughter, who loathed William and was estranged from her sister Mary.

The navy was manned by better trained officers, as the command of ships required technical knowledge. There were good schools of navigation in existence and more were founded at this time. The press-gang operating in the ports to get crews by force was unpopular and the conditions on board less than salubrious, being compared by Dr Johnson to 'a jail with the chance of being drowned'.[12] Many of the officers owed their rank to James, who had been Lord High Admiral after the Restoration of 1660 until the Test Act of 1673 forced him to resign as a Catholic convert. Even so, he remained afterwards in charge of the navy jointly with his brother Charles II. Many officers indebted to James remained loyal to him, though the policy of mixing the crews to take in a large number of Whigs loyal to William made it difficult for them to act independently at sea. The French won the naval battle of Beachy Head in June 1690, while William and James were in Ireland. It gave the French control of the

Channel, though they were unable to follow it up. The French plan had been to send their fleet to the Irish Sea in order to destroy William's transports and to isolate him in Ireland, but this was foiled by the Battle of the Boyne and James's flight from Ireland.[13] The battle fuelled suspicions of Jacobitism in the fleet. The English commander, Arthur Herbert, Earl of Torrington, had come over with the Prince of Orange in 1688, but his brother William Herbert, Marquis of Powis (Duke of Powis in the Jacobite peerage), was James's Lord Chamberlain at St-Germain and still received much of his English income through Torrington.[14] Torrington was arrested after this miscarriage and not employed again. Beachy Head was avenged by Edward Russell's naval victory at La Hogue in May 1692. It prevented a descent on England by James's army with the support of French troops and the French navy, which was awaited by 7000–8000 Jacobite troops raised in England, mostly Catholics and Nonjurors. Russell, who commanded the British navy, had come over with William in 1688, had been negotiating with the Stuart Court at St-Germain and was said to have promised James to keep out of the way while James's invasion sailed to England, provided the Dutch fleet had not joined Russell's fleet as it did before La Hogue. Russell's conduct was probably prompted by seeking reinsurance at St-Germain, should the invasion from France succeed. His failure to follow up his victory over the French, however, produced a storm in Parliament. Russell was replaced in command of the fleet by a commission consisting of two Tory admirals, Sir Ralph Delaval and Henry Killigrew, Jacobites who made proposals to Louis XIV through the Earl of Ailesbury for restoring James, and a third, Sir Clowdisley Shovell, a Whig opposed to James.

The loss of the Smyrna convoy to the French in 1693 represented the greatest naval disaster of the reign. The largest Anglo-Dutch commercial fleet sailing to England from Turkey was captured or destroyed by the French. Delaval and Killigrew, who were criticised for not sending ships out to get intelligence of the Smyrna convoy, blamed the loss on lack of co-operation on the part of the Dutch fleet. It led to Russell coming back as sole commander of the fleet, replacing the three admirals.[15] Though the French had lost control of the Channel, British shipping suffered greatly from the depredations of the Dunkirk and other French privateers and English merchants complained endlessly to Parliament about their losses due to lack of convoys. Nottingham, who had taken charge of the navy, was inexperienced in naval affairs and had to resign. A different strategy for attacking Louis in France produced the disaster of the landing in 1694 at Camaret Bay, adjoining Brest. The plan had been betrayed to James by John Churchill. Sir Winston Churchill, in his biography of his great ancestor, John Churchill, lst Duke of Marlborough, has sought to deny this. The conclusive evidence is in a note in James's own hand: 'May 4th, Lord Churchill informed the King of the design on Brest'.[16] The French were told, so that when the troops led by Talmash, an experienced Whig commander, landed, they found French batteries trained on them. Talmash was killed. The majority of British prisoners taken by the French opted to go and serve in James's army rather than to return to England.[17] Further bombardments of the French northern coasts broke a lot of windows but achieved little military result.[18]

In Flanders the Allies of the League of Ausgburg of 1688, the Emperor, Spain, Sweden, the Duke of Savoy, the Duke of Bavaria and other lesser German princes formed the Grand Alliance against France when the Dutch States and Britain joined them against Louis XIV. The reality was very different. The King of Denmark, the Electors of Brandenburg and Hanover and others agreed to provide troops in return for a subsidy from Britain. Thus began the system, which went on until the nineteenth century, of Britain purchasing the services of mercenaries to use in Europe, against Britons themselves in 1715–16 and 1745–46, and against the American colonists in the War of Independence. The coalition, projected in Britain as a crusade against popery and absolutism, contained the largest Catholic powers in Europe: the Empire and Spain (who had qualms about allying with William, a Calvinist), and several princes, such as the Duke of Savoy, who joined for separate interests. Some Lutheran states who furnished troops in exchange for money, such as Denmark and Hanover, were among the most autocratic in Europe.[19] The States General and William III, on Britain's behalf, agreed to support the Emperor's claim to the whole Spanish succession with far-reaching results, not grasped in England at the time. This policy went contrary to Tory belief in a blue-water strategy, concentrating on trade and sea power, as the only course serving British interests. There was an element of xenophobia in all this, but their belief that the interests of Britain, the greater power, were subordinated to those of the Dutch, the smaller power, had substance. Dislike of foreigners was not all-inclusive, for if the Tories hated the Dutch, they themselves were accused frequently of being too pro-French.

In 1691 William, at the head of 60 000 troops, failed to prevent Louis XIV from taking Mons, the strongest fortress in the Spanish Netherlands. He was the first monarch to lead the army in person since Henry VIII. In the struggle against Louis, he lacked the skilled administrators

and generals, who had enabled France to refine war in Flanders down to
a fine art. The French, moreover, had their bases near at hand, and
were able to live off the land.[20] Of the army commanded by William,
about 90 000 were British or Dutch, with 30 000 Brandenburgers, 12 000
from Saxony, 7000 Spaniards and 12 000 troops from the Emperor. It
was difficult to secure concerted action, and Spanish help was negligible.
In 1692 Namur fell to Louis, because it was believed the Dutch, the Spanish and the German allies were at loggerheads. At the Battle of Steinkirk
in the summer of 1692, British battalions had to bear the brunt of the
attack of the great French army, while the Dutch stood by. At the Battle
of Neerwinden or Landen in the summer of 1693, when the army was
commanded by Count Solms, William's kinsman, the Brandenburgers
and the Hanoverians were inactive and the British bore the brunt of the
fighting. Solms had no affection for the British and was indifferent to the
number of casualties, but his conduct was due to incompetence rather
than malice. Of the 130 000 troops involved on both sides, 23 000 died,
including Solms and, on the French side, Sarsfield, the Irish Jacobite
hero.[21]

10

THE ANGER OF PARLIAMENT, THE COUNTRY PARTY, COURTLY REFORMATION AND THE REFORM OF MANNERS

The series of military defeats and financial crises produced heated debates in Parliament. They had been unexpected, as the real state of operations had been censured or falsified in the *London Gazette*, the official newspaper.[1] The Whigs, who supported the war against France and projected themselves as the patriotic party, were dismayed. Others, such as Sir John Lowther of Lowther, a moderate Tory, who believed in the necessity of the struggle against France, were shocked at the lack of success in military operations. The leading Tories fell out with William III over the conduct of the war. Most of the Tories did not believe in taking part in warfare on the Continent at all, and they resented having to bear the brunt of the financial cost by way of the land tax. All this coincided with the emergence of a Country party led by Robert Harley and Paul Foley, former Presbyterians who went over to the Tories. This party was a mixture of independent or discontented Whigs and Tories, rather than the non-party organisation described by earlier historians.[2] The Country party included Sir Thomas Clarges and Sir Christopher Musgrave, Tories with Jacobite contacts.[3] It worked in with the investigations of a powerful Commission of Accounts, elected by ballot, to 'examine, take and state the public accounts' since William's invasion in 1688 and to make sure the vast sums voted for the war were not misappropriated. The Commissioners of Accounts were powerful and forced ministers to reveal much information, which had hitherto been kept secret.[4] They did not, however, manage to do what the Whigs did in the Exclusion crisis, namely to get Lists of secret-service pensions and the names of their recipients.[5] These were paid out of the Civil List, which also provided ministerial salaries and the cost of the Royal Household. The Civil List Act of 1697 [9 & 10 Wm. III cap. 23], however, increased William's Civil List to £700 000 a year out of tunnage (tax on wine) and poundage (tax on imported goods), and freed it from Parliamentary scrutiny hereafter.

Criticism of the conduct of the war continued. Rochester argued that the present military strategy was 'not suitable to the interest of England', while Carmarthen said it was 'not the way to put an end to the war', which was very unpalatable to William.[6] Musgrave thought England was being ruined for the sake of Flanders. Clarges declared that the army was for the defence of the kingdom, not for wars abroad, and that the Dutch, who supplied the army with butter and cheese, were the only ones to gain. He added that Cromwell's victorious army had cost £600 000 a year whereas William's cost £3 million a year.[7] The practices of Sir John Elwill, a Dissenter and factor for the Dutch in the West Country, were denounced by Sir Edward Seymour as producing a new pattern for the woollen trade, resulting in 'English stocks, English risks, English labours and Dutch profits'.[8] The Whigs supported the war in Flanders, but were reluctant to agree to the subordination of the English army there to Dutch officers. Goodwin Wharton, who was a Country Whig, unlike his brother Thomas, declared: 'we want no foreign officers, we have natives fit for employment. Nothing but an English army can preserve our liberties and property.'[9]

The dynastic question was still very much alive. Thomas Wharton, a leading Whig, had tried since 1690 to force the Tories out of office by imposing bills to compel them to abjure James II and 'the pretended Prince of Wales'. John Smith, a ministerialist Whig, for his part, pointed out that some Tory members of the government did not believe William was the rightful king but 'only de facto'.[10] As it was treason to criticise William directly, it was usual, for Tories especially, to criticise the Dutch instead. 'If you will discover a Tory or a Jacobite,' wrote the 3rd Earl of Shaftesbury, 'mention but the Dutch and you will discover them by their passionate railing.'[11] The Tories, wrote John Toland, a Whig publicist, could not damn King William, so they cursed the Dutch instead.[12] The Whigs, including those who had collaborated with James II and the Protestant Dissenters, apart from the Quakers, on the other hand, regarded William as the 'Great Deliverer' from popery and absolutism. The

Huguenots, victims of religious persecution themselves, were eager to persecute Roman Catholics in their turn. Jacobite pamphlets, on their side, denounced William's grants to his mistress Elizabeth Villiers and alleged homosexual relations with his Dutch favourites, William Bentinck, Earl of Portland and later with Arnold Joost van Keppel, Earl of Albemarle. William III's character hindered his English protagonists. Reserved and seclusive and suffering from asthma, he did not like Whitehall (which burnt down in 1698) and withdrew to Kensington Palace and Hampton Court in the company of his foreign advisers.

The many challenges to William's rule and right to rule, the military setbacks and endless demands for money, required a government publicity campaign to counter it. This took the form of the 'Courtly reformation', which presented William as a providential ruler (divine right by providence), who had a divine commission to protect the Protestant Church in England and to return the nation to its pristine faith, piety and virtue.[13] Divine right by providence was anathema to Jeremy Collier, a Nonjuror, who thought it would turn 'all Title into Force and Success' and 'make the Devil, if he should prevail, the Lord's anointed'.[14] Courtly reformation depicted William as the divinely appointed agent of moral reform, and by designating days for fasting and thanksgiving, portrayed the Royal Court as purged of sin and as the patron of the Church and the reformation of manners. It was promoted by a small group around William, who attempted to justify his regime by setting it in a Protestant and providential pattern in English history. It emphasised the concept of a godly prince, and moral reform was used by Burnet in his interpretation of history. Popery was said to be the source of moral laxity after the Restoration, so that the Revolution of 1688 presented a new opportunity for moral reform. James II blamed his own past sins for his misfortunes, but Burnet blamed the sins of Englishmen for all miscarriages and military defeats and equated sin with treason. Louis XIV was presented as Antichrist (at a time when he turned to religious devotion), and Versailles, rather than Rome, became the new Babylon. Burnet tried to enlist others, such as Bishops John Tillotson, Thomas Tenison, William Wake and Edward Stillingfleet, in this crusade, which was promoted by a torrent of Pastoral Letters and Visitations. Their most receptive audience, however, was not in Anglican churches but in dissenting meeting houses.[15] Bishop Burnet, its chief instigator and a man of intelligence and learning, never made the impact in English politics his role in the Revolution should have given him. This was probably because he was a Scot, a former Presbyterian, something of a buffoon, or owing to the burning of his Pastoral Letter on the orders of Parliament. His physical appearance and manner were unprepossessing:

> A big-boned northern priest,
> With pliant body and with brawny fist,
> Whose mighty blows the dusty cushions thrash.
> And make the trembling pulpit's wainscoat crash.[16]

Courtly reformation went alongside the movement embodied in the Societies for the Reformation of Manners, which many historians have regarded as independent and critical of William's regime. Many MPs connected with the movement espoused Country principles and were in opposition to the Court. Some societies were even suspected of sedition and Jacobite sympathies. Moral reformers urged stricter laws against drunkenness, prostitution, and profane swearing. Some magistrates led their own campaign against vice in their localities. Most Englishmen, however, did not wish to revive the puritan terror of Cromwell's day and Parliament was wise enough not to attempt to legislate against sin.[17]

As part of the 'Country' campaign and concern about preserving Parliament from placemen and court manipulation, bills were introduced to limit the number of office-holders in Parliament and to make Parliaments triennial, so that there should be a general election every three years. The Place Bill brought in in December 1692 excluded from the Commons MPs who accepted places of profit under the Crown after being elected. It passed easily in the Commons. The King and his ministers were deeply hostile to it, as there were at least 100 placemen in the Commons whose presence was essential to carry on government business. When it came before the Lords, Court Whigs, Court Tories and many bishops were against it. After tremendous lobbying and much bribery by the Court, it was rejected by 47 to 45.[18] The King vetoed a new Place Bill, which had passed both Houses in December 1693, as well as the Triennial Bill, which had the support of Shrewsbury. Charles II had used the royal veto only once in the whole of his reign, and William was using it twice in two years! Country discontent swelled and Robert Harley declared, ominously, that if the King could veto bills, the House could withhold supplies.[19] William eventually yielded to Shrewsbury and allowed the Triennial Act to pass in 1694 [6 & 7 Wm. and Mary cap. 2]. This provided that a Parliament should be held once every three years at least and that there should be a general election every three years. It differed radically from the Triennial Act of 1664, which made provision for Parliament meeting at least once in three years rather than for a new election every three years. Frequent general elections after 1694 prevented too strong a hold on small boroughs by government patronage or private patrons. It kept 'the rage of party' at fever pitch, each side courting the electors.

The irritation of the King at these events was turned to sorrow by the death of his Queen of smallpox in 1694. Though he had been patriarchal and undemonstrative towards her in life, he showed real grief at her death. Her beauty and charm had been a valuable asset. She could not heal the breach between William and Princess Anne as she was on the worst of terms with her sister, but she did build bridges with many others. She was useful too for her skill at handling ecclesiastical patronage, which was left to her. She stood in contrast to Mary of Modena, who had a mind of her own and would not tolerate her husband's infidelities. Mary's chaplain, Bishop Burnet, had persuaded her it was her wifely duty to yield to her husband in all things and, though she had a shrewder knowledge of English politics than he did, she bowed to his judgement and allowed herself to be overruled. Her death left William III more isolated in England than before, and looking more like an usurper.

11

THE WHIG JUNTO, THE FOUNDATION OF THE BANK OF ENGLAND AND THE FINANCIAL REVOLUTION

The 2nd Earl of Sunderland came back into favour as chief adviser to William III. A Whig and an Exclusionist, he was regarded by many as James II's evil genius because, as Chief Minister, he had implemented James's policies of religious toleration and remodelling the corporations before the elections to the proposed 1688 Parliament. Despite this, Sunderland had no reservations about William's title to the Crown and with his protegé, Henry Guy, Secretary to the Treasury since 1679, managed the Court party better than anyone. Sunderland in 1694 argued that the mixed ministries had been unfair since the Whigs and Tories were 'not equal in relation to this government' as the first 'may be made for it', while 'not a quarter of the other ever can'.[1] The Whig junto profoundly distrusted Sunderland as one as ready to do William III's dirty work as he had been to do James II's. Worse still from his rivals' point of view, Sunderland was an extremely able politician. Edward Russell put it in a nutshell: 'when the fox is abroad look to your lambs'.[2] The political scene was changing at this time. Burnet noticed the switch in Whig and Tory traditional roles: 'By an odd reverse the Whigs, who were now most employed argued for the prerogative, while the Tories seemed zealous for public liberty.'[3] Though Tories were not excluded, the balance shifted towards the Whigs. Charles Montagu, a very able young Whig, became Chancellor of the Exchequer, while John Smith replaced

Sir Edward Seymour at the Treasury and Russell came back as First Lord of the Admiralty. The government was dominated by Montagu, Somers, the Lord Keeper, Shrewsbury, the senior Secretary of State, Thomas Wharton, Comptroller of the Household (who was as much loved by the voters as he was disliked by the King because of his easygoing familiarity), and Russell. They were the nucleus of the Whig junto, a tight-knit group, who dominated politics for so long. Montagu wrote: 'We should have but one common interest, the same friends and the same enemies. No measures to be kept, no friendship maintained, with those that are at defiance with the rest.'[4]

The Whigs were better organised and disciplined than the Tories, who included many country squires with estates to look after and who tended to arrive late and leave early in each session. Montagu, more than anyone, was responsible for the financial revolution, which transformed public finances and was driven by the enormous cost of the war. Taxes multiplied, including taxes on windows, marriages, births and burials, very unpopular and not yielding large sums. The most profitable and easiest tax to levy was the land tax, based on rents, ranging from 1 shilling to 4 shillings in the pound. Roman Catholics and Nonjurors paid double. This was more difficult to evade than taxing property and it meant that the landed classes, the section of the population most opposed to the war, paid for it. England became one of the most heavily taxed countries in the world, and the increase in revenue was due to higher taxes rather than to economic growth.[5] In 1693–94 Montagu set up the Million Lottery on the security of the salt duties and the additional excise granted for 16 years, offering 'fortune tickets', some worth £1000 and some £500 a year. In April 1694 he secured the passage of an ingenious bill to provide for a loan of £1 200 000 at 8 per cent interest and to allow for further borrowings on the security of taxes and to incorporate the subscribers into a Bank.[6] This was the foundation of the Bank of England and was inspired Dutch financial expertise. The Bank, which was authorised to deal in bullion and bills of exchange, proved a spectacular success and within two years it was circulating £1¾ million in paper money. The national debt which it created gave its stockholders a secure and profitable investment, in which gradually many sections of the community participated,[7] including earlier Tory opponents. The Bank of England helped to develop the securities market so that the state did not have to pay the principal and interest on its debt. Remittances to pay the army abroad remained largely with powerful financial syndicates, such as those of Sir Stephen Evance and the Herne brothers (all MPs), though the Treasury transferred some of the business to the Bank. It gave a huge vested interest to the Revolution settlement and it did much for the Whig cause. The Bank was backed by leading Dissenters in the City of London, many of them Huguenots of the third generation settled in England. Robert Harley, who came from a Nonconformist family, was later to reflect that the Dissenters 'acted against all their principles and the liberties of the nation'.[8]

The long-term effect of the financial revolution was an acceleration in the development of the administrative sector of the state which had been taking place since 1660, and it led to a great increase in the powers of those raising taxes, of the Treasury and of the Customs and the Excise. The Excise grew in importance in state finance under Cromwell in the 1650s. It was unpopular because its officers had the right to search, which caused popular disturbances. Retained after the Restoration of 1660 because of its profitability, it was too obnoxious, however, to turn it into a general Excise in 1666. It was expanded as a tax on beer, wine and spirits after 1689.[9] The war made the state the largest borrower and spender, as well as the largest single employer. The biggest increase in jobs was in the Customs and in the Excise. The Excise was the most efficient branch of the revenue out of the two services. England had a more efficient taxation system than France and its ability to raise credit on the security of future taxes enabled it to become a world power in time. On the other hand, the war and foreign affairs departments were rudimentary compared to those in France. The war absorbed 10–15 per cent of national expenditure.[10] The financial revolution gave the state an efficient borrowing capacity, but it needed an efficient taxation system to back it up. It enabled Britain to mount military operations on a vast scale all over the world and to pay for them on credit. The Bank of England, the raising of loans on the security of taxation thus anticipating the revenue, had the long-term effect of making the King and government much less dependent on Parliament and provided ample funds to manage and corrupt Parliament. The government obtained money not from resources but from debts.

Greater London had expanded enormously, though the population of the City declined after the Plague and the Great Fire in the reign of Charles II, and most of the capital mobilised by the government came from and around London.[11] Harley tried in vain to set up a Land Bank as a rival, offering loans to the state on the security of rents from land, which was passed as a bill in 1698 with strong Tory backing, but which failed as a Bank. The City of London was very much a tale of two cities. The Bank of England and the directors of the large joint-stock companies (except the

Old East India Company) were dominated by the Whigs, many of them Dissenters. They were closely identified with war finance after 1690. Most of them were aldermen of London, who were chosen for life and had to have a property qualification of £10 000. On the other hand, the smaller merchants and traders,who dominated the Common Council (councillors elected in each of the wards), and the Common Hall (the livery, or members of the City guilds, assembled to elect the London MPs, Sheriffs and other officers), the popular part of the City, which had been the stronghold of the Whigs, had veered to Toryism.[12] They supported the Church of England and protectionism. They cast themselves as protectors of the economic interests of ordinary freemen and resented non-freemen and foreigners, such as the Huguenots or the refugees from the Palatinate in Germany, practising trades in the City. When Tory mobs rioted in London, they sacked the meeting houses of Dissenters.[13] Samuel Travers, a placeman and an MP, left a bequest to erect a statue 'to the glorious memory of my master William III' in the precincts of City of London. It was indicative of its change of mood that the City of London would never allow it to be put up within its boundaries.[14]

The war produced another problem for the government: the lamentable state of the coinage. Large quantities of silver were being exported from clipping the unmilled edge of silver coins, which debased the coinage. In 1695 a completely new coinage was decided upon, arranged in collaboration between Charles Montagu, Somers, Locke, William Lowndes (who succeeded Henry Guy as chief Secretary to the Treasury) and Isaac Newton as Master of the Mint. This was sound in the long run, but its immediate effect was a shortage of money which made it difficult for people to buy the bare necessities of life. It was not until 1699 that the state of the coin was less than catastrophic and that paper money, the government's preferred option, was generally accepted.[15]

12

THE FENWICK PLOT AND THE ASSASSINATION PLOT OF 1696, THE PEACE OF RYSWICK, MOVES TO RESTORE THE STUARTS

There was no freedom of speech or of the press for Jacobites, and printers as well as authors of Jacobite literature could be put to death. The lapsing of the Licensing Act in 1695, contrary to what Macaulay asserted, did not produce freedom of the press. Governments prosecuted under the law of seditious libels and had wide powers to search and seize copy under general warrants. More newspapers were produced in William's reign, but they were subdued, unlike the newspapers during the Exclusion crisis, after an earlier Licensing Act had lapsed. Though the Licensing Act was not renewed in 1695, political issues were not discussed in newspapers as freely as they were during the reign of Queen Anne (in whose reign no Jacobite was put to death).[1] It was harder to curb speech, and John Hampden lamented this situation: 'we are entirely unsettled as to the government. The king's title, and the legality of it, are as publicly disputed, and with as little fear of punishment, as any point of natural philosophy in the schools of Oxford, or any moot case of law by the students of the Temple.'[2]

Despite draconian measures taken against Jacobitism, Jacobite pamphlets and literature, with the connivance of sympathetic printers and distributors, were published and made a powerful impact. In 1695, Robert Ferguson wrote one of the most skilful pieces of Jacobite propaganda ever produced and one which greatly angered King William and his ministers. This was *A Brief Account of Some of the Late Encroachments and Depredations of the Dutch upon the English*. It accused the Dutch of stripping the country of coin, leaving English merchant ships unprotected, snubbing English army officers while rewarding the Dutch, and concluded that the Prince of Orange 'had no title to be King'.

The crisis of the recoinage and the general discontent it produced coincided in 1696 with a plan for a Jacobite rising in England to take place after troops promised by Louis XIV (the last time Louis agreed to provide military assistance on English soil to restore the Stuarts). Persons of the highest rank, as the Duke of Berwick reported, had engaged to take part in the rising once troops from France, Louis's and James's, had landed, as without military support they would be arrested before they could act. This was an essential point Louis XIV did not seem to grasp. Sir George Barclay, an experienced army officer who had fought with Viscount Dundee in Scotland in 1689, came over to England to investigate the situation. He devised a plan, unbeknownst to the leaders of the proposed main rising, to kidnap and kill William III as he went hunting in Richmond Park. Sir John Fenwick, who was principally involved in organising the rising, and other leading participants either knew nothing or disapproved of the Assassination Plot and would have nothing to do with it, but its discovery ruined them and their plans. Barclay escaped, but his accomplices were either executed or kept in prison for life without a trial, which was illegal. Before the Trials for Treason Act of 1696 [7 & 8 Wm. III cap. 31], persons arrested for treason were not told what they were accused of and had little opportunity to defend themselves. The Act, passed under Tory and Country Whig pressure, provided that the accused should have a copy of the indictment against them, but not of the names of the witnesses. They should be allowed counsel and witnesses for the defence. There must be two witnesses at least for the prosecution. Anyone attempting to assassinate the king or queen or caught in counterfeiting the coin was excluded from its provisions. Peers were to be tried by the whole House of Lords only. Sir John Friend, a wealthy London brewer and a former MP, the commander and paymaster of the London Jacobite regiment, had not been involved in the Assassination Plot, but he was excluded from the benefits of the Trials for Treason Act on a technicality. He was executed at Tyburn in April 1696. In his dying speech he declared his belief 'that, as no foreign power, so neither any domestic power can alienate our allegiance. For it is altogether new and unintelligible to me that the King's subjects can depose or dethrone him on any account.'[3] William had a personal grudge against Sir John Fenwick, who had been a colonel in the Dutch army in 1675 and had criticised the Dutch for being bad payers of his troops. Fenwick was to command a regiment of horse in the 1696 rising, but the government lacked enough legal proofs (it had only one witness against him) to prosecute him in a court of law. Disregarding the recent statute regulating trials for treason it had recently passed, Parliament proceeded against Sir John Fenwick by bill of attainder in Parliament. It was the most notorious political trial of the time. Refusing to save himself by turning King's evidence against his fellow conspirators, Fenwick disclosed the dealings of the Whig junto with James II at St-Germain, naming Shrewsbury, Russell, Godolphin and Sunderland, which infuriated the King. Sir Richard Onslow, a country Whig, opposed Fenwick's attainder as illegal and his grandson, Arthur Onslow (Speaker of the House of Commons in Sir Robert Walpole's time), wrote subsequently that most people thought Fenwick had told the truth.[4] The ministers named by Fenwick denied all and hurried along his execution. Godolphin was subsequently dismissed. Shrewsbury, however, would not brazen it out indefinitely and he retired to Italy for health reasons, choosing this location, as he said, because no Protestant country was blessed with sunshine.

The discovery of the Assassination Plot had a devastating effect on the Jacobites and strengthened the position of William III. For the first time the Tories had to take an oath acknowledging that William was the 'rightful and lawful' king and to abjure James II and the 'pretended Prince of Wales' if they wanted to stay in Parliament or to hold national or local office. A large number of Tories refused to swear at first. Most did so in the end, as the Royalists had done during the Interregnum on the ground that oaths taken under duress were not binding. They were forced to take these oaths periodically until the death of William III. When Lord Feversham told the Duke of Leeds (Danby) he could not swear the Prince of Wales was 'pretended' as he had seen him being born, Leeds persuaded him to comply, as the word 'pretended' did not refer to the facts of the birth but to the abrogation of the child's claim to the throne by Parliament.[5]

William III's retaking of Namur from the French in 1695 was the one major victory on the continent of Europe in his reign. The death in that year of the maréchal de Luxembourg, Louis's best general, made France less invincible than hitherto. Afterwards both sides felt exhausted by the long war and they began to think of peace. The King was childless and his dislike of Princess Anne was mutual. There is a good deal of evidence to suggest that he had never believed in the 'warming-pan' story and that he seriously considered a Stuart restoration after his own death. In July 1696 he made overtures to the Stuart court at St-Germain, offering to make the Prince of Wales his heir provided he could retain the throne for the rest of his life. It was James's queen, Mary of Modena, who was responsible for rejecting the proposal on the grounds that the son could not succeed during the lifetime of his father.[6] In September 1697 the Treaty of Ryswick was signed which made peace between Britain and France. It forced the French to recognise William III (who had hitherto been invariably called William *le Prince d'Orange* by the French) as King of England. William sent Bentinck, the Earl of Portland, his most trusted adviser, as ambassador to France. Louis had treated James and his family in exile with chivalry and generosity. The château of St-Germain, the ancient seat of the Kings of France until 1685, was placed at James's disposal. With funds from France and those sent by his British supporters, James II was in a better financial position than Charles II in exile had been. He and his queen presided over a splendid example of a baroque Court, with wide powers of patronage, in art and music especially.[7] Louis XIV had a particular regard for Mary of Modena and would not have his Stuart friends humiliated. Most of the French Court was pro-Jacobite and was hostile to Portland. In these circumstances, Portland could not cut as imposing a figure as he had hoped and he did not remain long in France.

The peace created even greater problems for William III in England. There were £5½ million in debts owing, including £2 million due to the army, £2½ million due to the navy, as well as subsidies to German allies and Denmark.[8] Soldiers and seamen had not been paid regularly and there were suspicions of financial corruption. Lord Ranelagh, an Irish peer and an MP, helped himself to public funds on an even greater scale than he had in the reign of Charles II, until he was expelled from Parliament in 1703 for misappropriating £72 000 as Paymaster-General of the army.[9] Edward Russell, Earl of Orford, Treasurer of the navy, was accused of making a vast fortune out of his office and was forced to resign.

At this time there was not only a Country platform (an agreed programme of reforms to which Tories and opposition Whigs alike subscribed), as there was post-1715, but an effective Country party, acting as a coherent force in Parliament. They concurred on many issues, often for different reasons. Independent Whigs were as critical of the new regime in England and of some Protestant rulers in Europe as the Tories were. In a very influential pamphlet *Account of the State of Denmark* (1694), which covered Hanover too, Robert Molesworth, a Country Whig, had pointed out the risk to English freedom from absolutist and obscurantist Protestant rulers. In fact, Lutheranism could be a shorter route to absolutism than Roman Catholicism. Like George I after him, William was interested in a professional army only and neglected the militia. The members of the Country party could agree on disbanding the army, relying on the militia and curbing financial corruption, but they parted company on other issues. Sir Richard Cocks, a Country Whig, upheld Revolution Principles and denounced 'priestcraft' and the harassment of Dissenters. He seemed to prefer the Huguenots and the Dutch to his own countrymen,[10] all anathema to Tories. A group of Whig radical intellectuals in the 1690s believed all subjects had natural rights to life, liberty and property, which no government should infringe without due process of law. They regarded as absurd the notion that the labouring poor should have any voice in decision-making in the state. Only men of property had the education, time, and economic independence to cultivate the civic virtues required by men wielding legislative power. They sought to limit the powers of the monarchy, but saw sovereignty as in the King, Lords and Commons, not in the people. Many of these Whigs were anticlerical and they were anxious to curb the social, economic and political power of the Church of England.[11]

The one point on which all sections of the Country party could agree was on disbanding the standing army in terms of peace. In December 1697 Robert Harley moved that all land forces raised since 1680 should be disbanded and paid off, effectively reducing the army to its size in 1680 – it was to be cut to 7000 men. The Dutch guards which had been with William since 1688 were to go, despite earnest pleas from the King.[12] Disbanded officers were to receive a gratuity and disbanded soldiers were to be allowed to practise a trade. The militia was to be made effective once more.[13] The debate was conducted not only in Parliament but out of doors in the great 'No Standing Army' controversy.[14] This was dominated by the Country party led by Robert Harley and Paul Foley. Some of its most gifted protagonists such as Robert Molesworth, John Trenchard and Walter Moyle were Whigs, but the rank and file were mostly Tories.[15] To the Tories a standing army stood for the New Model Army, Cromwell and the domination of Parliament by the army. To independent Whigs, it represented the praetorian guard overthrowing the liberties of ancient Rome. Moyle and Trenchard, in *An Argument shewing that a standing army is inconsistent with a free government, and absolutely destructive to the constitution of the English Monarchy* (1697), maintained that a mercenary army disturbed the delicate balance between King, Lords and Commons. The militia was the only legitimate army as the people would never oppress themselves. They denounced the apostasy of those Whigs who had advocated the disbandment of Charles II's few Guards, but who were now happy to keep 20 000 men in time of peace. The reduction of the army coincided with a successful Place Bill in 1700, tacked (attached) to the land tax, so that the Lords could not reject it, making the Commissioners of Customs and Excise ineligible to sit in Parliament. William had no option but to give royal assent as he needed the money and it passed into law [12 & 13 Wm. III cap. 10]. The enquiry into Irish forfeitures declared void William's extravagant grants to his favourites and the Resumption Bill of February 1699 annulled Irish forfeitures. The Peace of Ryswick may have been only a temporary cessation in hostilities, but it deprived William of the argument that any opposition to the war against France was unpatriotic, and it enabled the Country opposition to get its way.

13

THE SPANISH SUCCESSION AND THE ACT OF SETTLEMENT

Meanwhile, William III was preoccupied with the succession of Carlos II, the ailing king of Spain, whose death without a male heir threatened to start new conflicts in Europe. By the first Barrier Treaty in 1698 between the Dutch Republic and Spain, the Dutch were allowed to garrison some towns in the Spanish Netherlands to provide a 'barrier' against French invasion. Consulting only Portland and Keppel, Earl of Albemarle, his younger Dutch favourite, William concluded two Partition Treaties. The first, in 1698, gave Spain, the Spanish Netherlands and the Spanish overseas Empire to the Electoral Prince of Bavaria, while Naples and Sicily went to the Dauphin, Louis XIV's heir, and Milan to Archduke Charles of Austria. The Bavarian claimant died in 1699 and the second Partition Treaty of 1700 awarded Spain, the Spanish Netherlands and the Indies to Archduke Charles, while Naples, Sicily and the Tuscan ports were granted to the Dauphin. This was done in order to prevent another war and the intention was laudable. All these princes had legitimate claims to the Spanish dominions. While it gave territorial acquisitions to France which would have been of great advantage to the French Levant (Mediterranean) fleet, Britain had nothing. William had not consulted his English ministers, Somers, Orford (Russell) and Halifax (Charles Montagu), but had merely informed them. Somers, the Lord Chancellor, had issued a blank commission for the second treaty and affixed the Great Seal to it during the sitting of Parliament without any reference to it.[1] Carlos II, who had not been consulted on the planned share-out of his dominions, wanted to preserve them intact and, in order to do so, made a will leaving

everything to Philip, Duke of Anjou, Louis XIV's grandson, with a pro-
viso that Spain and France were not to be united. This settlement was
accepted by the Dutch and the British at first. Tories hoped that Philip
would act in future as a Spaniard rather than as a French prince. The
King was still preoccupied with the royal succession in England. Princess
Anne had had a large number of children either stillborn or who died
young. Even before the death of the young, sickly Duke of Gloucester,
Anne's last child, in 1700, William met Sophia, Electress of Hanover, at
Loo in 1699 to discuss the succession. She advised him to recognise the
Prince of Wales, James Francis Edward, as his heir provided he conformed to the Church of England. James would not hear of the Prince
abandoning what he regarded as the only true faith and he kept a close
watch on his son lest William attempted to have him kidnapped.[2]

A separate development was a large number of persons, MPs and peers
from England and Scotland, going to the Stuart court at St-Germain to
ask James to allow the prince to be brought up as an Anglican. They
included Lord Windsor, Sir John Parsons, an influential alderman and
sometime Lord Mayor of London, and Fergus Grahme, brother of James
Grahme MP, who carried this very proposal from Sir Christopher
Musgrave.[3] This would have been a very popular solution, with the
Tories especially, but they had no more success that William III had had.
It does show, however, the importance attached by both sides to the direct hereditary succession and that the devolution of the Crown agreed
by the Convention in 1689 was not regarded as immutable. The royal
succession was a thorny problem as, the Duke of Devonshire wrote
privately, 'the Prince of Wales must be kept out' and yet 'the nation will
not submit to any more foreigners'.[4]

The election to the Parliament which met in February 1701 had a small
Tory majority. Robert Harley, elected Speaker, met the King in secret
and promised that a bill would be passed settling the succession on Electress Sophia and the House of Brunswick. Harley needed to win over
only a few Tories to get it through, as the Whigs supported it. Godolphin,
the minister most resembling the Vicar of Bray (the clergyman, celebrated
in song, for going over to each of the winning sides in turn during the
Civil Wars), came back at the head of the Treasury and Montagu was
made Baron Halifax. Rochester, the senior Tory politician, who never
recognised William as more than *de facto* king, became Lord-Lieutenant
of Ireland. He was bold enough to tell William 'that princes must not only
hear good advice, but must take it'.[5] On 15 February 1701 Jack Howe, a
leading Tory, opened the attack on the junto for the Partition Treaties.

Proceedings began with the impeachment of William's dismissed ministers, Portland, Somers, Orford and Halifax, for their share in concluding the Partition Treaties without consulting Parliament. The monarchy was not as yet a constitutional monarchy and the royal prerogative entitled William to conclude treaties without submitting them to Parliament. He had kept these treaties hitherto as secret as Charles II had kept the Treaty of Dover secret. But circumstances had changed. The Nine Years War had cost unprecedented sums voted by Parliament to maintain a vast army and a large navy, and it was reasonable for Parliament to expect a say in deciding the future of Europe and how to promote British interests. The impeachment of Portland did not proceed, perhaps in deference to the King. The House of Lords, in which the Whigs had a majority, threw out the other impeachments. William upped the stakes by putting before the Commons a supposed letter from Melfort to his brother, the Duke of Perth, intimating that an invasion to restore James was afoot in France. The Anglican Earl of Middleton had long replaced Melfort as James's Secretary of State at St-Germain, there was no such planned invasion and even at the time many suspected it was a forgery. Like the warming-pan story, however, it was a useful invention and served a turn. The court of Hanover watched events in England closely. It was reported to Electress Sophia that 'whatever people may have in their hearts, few will appear so open at this time as to declare for St. Germain'.[6] On 1 March 1701 Lord Spencer, grandson of the 2nd Earl and a Whig, moved that the succession should be settled in Electress Sophia and the House of Brunswick. Bonet, the Prussian envoy, wrote that it was the command of the King that it should be brought in. This ensured that the Act of Settlement was passed. Bonet commented that the Tories did not attend when they felt powerless, but did so when they could influence any part of it.[7] They were able to exact a heavy price and made parts of it an indictment of William's reign. The limitations proposed by Harley and the Tories were supported by some independent Whigs.[8] Harley moved that the Commons should consider limitations on the powers of the Crown first. Sir John Bolles, the clown of the House, who showed signs of mental instability and was afterwards committed as a lunatic, was put in the chair of the committee. William, Lord Cowper, wrote subsequently that Bolles was put in the chair by the Tories to show 'their contempt and aversion' for the Bill.[9] The only Tory to speak against the Bill as such (Bonet reported) was John Granville, brother to the Earl of Bath. The Act [12 & 13 Wm. III cap. 2] was meant to come into force on the death of Anne, though some thought it should do so immediately. The limitations were direct criticisms of William. No foreign national was to be allowed to hold office, sit in Parliament or to be able to receive grants from the Crown. No foreigner would be able to be a member of the Privy Council, which was to resume the primordial role taken over by the Cabinet. No MP would be able to hold civil or military office or to be given grants of land by the Crown (a provision which would make future management of Parliament impossible). A future Hanoverian monarch would be unable to leave England without the consent of Parliament (William had spent a large part of the year in the Dutch Netherlands), or to wage war on behalf of foreign dominions without the consent of Parliament. A royal pardon should no longer be pleadable in cases of impeachment. No king or queen should be a Roman Catholic or marry a Roman Catholic. The tradition that the Act of Settlement was passed by one vote only cannot be proved or disproved as the crucial division in the Commons would have been in the committee of the whole House and, therefore, unrecorded in the *Commons Journals*. Most of these limitations were repealed on the accession of George I, with the exception of the clause giving judges security of tenure and the crucial clauses barring Roman Catholics from the succession.

In a campaign masterminded by Wharton, the Whigs counter-attacked vigorously. The Kentish Petitioners and others sent petitions and instructions to MPs demanding the dissolution of the present Parliament and asserting strong support for the King and his Allies against France. These instructions to MPs were published in 1701 under the title of *The Electors Right Asserted*. This was denounced by the Tories as a violation of the rights of Parliament. In response, Whig pamphlets exhorted the Tories to fulfil their traditional role by defending the royal prerogative rather than posing as the champions of the rights of the Commons.[10] The *Legion Memorial*, a clever piece of journalism by Daniel Defoe, one of Monmouth's rebels, called for war against France and accused Tory MPs of being pensioners of France, a charge not supported by any evidence in French sources. Most Tories, Rochester especially, wanted to avoid war against France if they possibly could. Although France and Austria were already engaged in hostilities, this did not mean Britain had to be involved. Neutrality was made more difficult when Louis, acting on behalf of his grandson, sent troops to the Spanish Netherlands to expel the Dutch garrisons from Antwerp, Mons and Namur, thus undoing what had been fought for in the Nine Years War. In August–September 1701 a Grand Alliance was concluded at The Hague between the

Emperor, the King of Great Britain and the States General for supporting the Hapsburg rights to the Spanish succession and to constitute a barrier for the Dutch in the Spanish Netherlands, stating that the Crowns of France and Spain must never be united and renewing the 1689 alliance with the Dutch.[11] War was made inevitable, as far as England was concerned, when James II died in September 1701 and Louis recognised the Prince of Wales as James III. He was not recognised as King of England *per se*, but his claim to the English throne was acknowledged.[12] Disregarding these subtleties, Britain declared war against France. The second, more Whiggish, 1701 Parliament, which met early in 1702, attainted the 'pretended Prince of Wales' and imposed another oath declaring William to be the 'rightful' and 'lawful' king. In February 1702 William III's horse 'Sorrel' threw him as it stumbled on a molehill. William broke his collarbone and died on 8 March 1702. Jacobites toasted the mole as 'the little gentleman in the black velvet' and rejoiced.

It was too late, as the mechanisms set about by the Dutch king to exclude James III were in place, never to be reversed. Bevill Higgons, the Jacobite poet, urged idle courtiers to

> Mourn for the mighty sums by him mis-spent
> Those prodigally given, those idly lent;
> Mourn for the Statues, and Tapestry too.
> From *Windsor* gutted to aggrandise *Loo*.[13]

14

THE WAR OF THE SPANISH SUCCESSION, THE DEATH OF QUEEN ANNE AND THE HANOVERIAN SUCCESSION

A detailed study of Queen Anne's reign falls outside the bounds of this volume. Suffice it to say that the country rejoiced at the accession in 1702 of Queen Anne, whose heart, as she proclaimed, was 'entirely English'. She had obtained a secret agreement from her half-brother James III not to press his claim while she lived.[1] Party struggles continued as fierce as ever, with each party creating its own support in the electorate. At first the Queen favoured the Tories. She refused, however, to rely on one party only and continued mixed ministries. The war against France and her close friendship with Sarah Duchess of Marlborough ensured that the Duke of Marlborough, the greatest military commander of his age, and Godolphin, the ablest financial minister, governed virtually jointly for nearly 20 years. The war against France (the War of the Spanish Succession, 1702–13) seemed to have its own impetus. Marlborough's victory at Blenheim in August 1704, usually regarded as one of the finest victories by the British army, stopped Louis XIV from overrunning Germany. Successful war, however, was not as yet a factor in forging British identity, for the Tories deplored all Marlborough's victories.[2] They disapproved of taking part in continental wars at all, and wanted a blue-water strategy, concentrating on trade and sea power. Marlborough and his commanders made huge fortunes out of the war. He and his Duchess made no distinction between public money and their own.[3] Military and naval officers, army contractors and financiers, who handled remittances to pay the troops, bought seats in Parliament and Parliamentary patronage at the expense of the country gentlemen who were paying for the war. This was anathema to the Tories. Foreign rulers, including the Elector of Hanover, who hired out their subjects as cannon fodder, received large subsidies from Britain, although they did not always field the number of troops British taxpayers had financed. Allies received various favours besides: England paid a subsidy of £150 000 to Portugal and one of £160 000 to Savoy in 1703, while Austria was allowed to raise a loan of £250 000 on the London capital market.[4] The Parliamentary Accounts Commission of 1713, which investigated frauds in the contracts for supplying the army with bread, clothing and forage for the horses, was dominated by Tory partisanship, but it nevertheless revealed fraudulent practices. Its recommendations, unimplemented after 1714, foreshadowed the Economical Reform in the 1780s.[5]

Tories were further frustrated by the growing numbers and influence of Protestant Dissenters, who evaded the provisions of the Test Act by taking the Sacrament in an Anglican Church once a year or occasionally, the Occasional Conformists. This was regarded by them as blasphemous and was likened by George Granville, Lord Lansdowne, the 1st Lord Bath's nephew, as 'those followers of Judas, who come to the Lord's supper to sell and betray him'.[6] Yet the best chance to ban Occasional Conformity in 1704 was foiled by the management of Robert Harley, who prevented its being passed as a tack to a money bill, a device often used in William's reign. The war went on and each victory of the Duke of Marlborough was meant to be the last. Marlborough, the victor of Blenheim, Ramillies, Oudenarde and Malplaquet, an English duke, a Prince of the Holy Roman Empire, bestrode Europe like a colossus. He appeared to think he had a divine right to govern Britain. At Malplaquet in August 1709, however, the carnage was so terrible it shocked most people. Tory hatred for the Duke of Marlborough cannot be overestimated. On the other hand, Marlborough was and remained a hero in the Whig pantheon.

While Britain triumphed in the Low Countries, the war was going badly in Spain, where Castilians wanted Philip V as their king rather than Archduke Charles, the Allies' candidate. When James Stanhope and his whole army were taken prisoner by the French at Brihuega in 1710 there was little hope of deposing Philip V, yet the Whigs in 1711 made 'No peace without Spain' their battle cry. In any case, as Archduke Charles succeeded as Emperor, making him King of Spain would have re-created the empire of Charles V rather than maintained the balance of power in

Europe, which was what the Allies were supposed to be doing. It was stalemate. Marlborough and Godolphin, supported almost exclusively by the Whigs, seemed unable or unwilling to make peace. This is probably because George of Brunswick, Electress Sophia's eldest son, was implacably opposed to peace with France. Queen Anne, for her part, had grown tired of the Duchess of Marlborough's ceaseless requests for her family and irascible temperament and this weakened the Duke of Marlborough's influence in England.

The trial of Dr Henry Sacheverell, a High Tory clergyman, in 1710 for a sermon entitled 'In peril of False Brethren', denouncing the Protestant Dissenters and reviving the doctrines of hereditary right and non-resistance, caused a political crisis for the Marlborough–Godolphin administration. Sacheverell was invited to preach in St Paul's Cathedral on 5 November (the traditional day for Whig celebrations of the discovery of the Gunpowder Plot and the landing of William of Orange). Before a packed congregation, containing many Jacobites and Nonjurors, he came, in the words of Geoffrey Holmes, not to praise the Revolution but to bury it. The chief danger to the Church of England, Sacheverell declared, was not from its acknowledged enemies but from its pretended friends, the Occasional Conformists, who profaned her altars in order to get into office. The Church of England, he went on, would lose all distinctive character and would be transformed into a 'heterogeneous mixture' of persons united only by Protestantism; and Protestantism, as he reminded the congregation, was only one aspect of the Church of England. Having failed 'to carry the Conventicle into the Church' these false brethren were resolved 'to bring the Church into the Conventicle'. Among them, as he made clear, were Gilbert Burnet, Bishop of Salisbury. He further attacked politicians who had deserted the Church and 'the crafty insidiousness of such wily Volpones'. 'Volpone' (the fox) was the nickname given to Lord Treasurer Godolphin, a former Tory.[7]

The Government and its Whig junto supporters were outraged. They proceeded to impeach Sacheverell in Parliament. In the course of the debates during the trial (February–March 1710), Wharton had abandoned the warming-pan story, admitted the legitimacy of James's son and based the Queen's right firmly on parliamentary sanction.[8] Nicholas Lechmere, a prominent Whig MP, reaffirmed Revolution principles:

The nature of our constitution is that of a limited monarchy, wherein the supreme power was – by mutual consent and not by accident – limited and lodged in more hands but one.... The consequence of such a form of government are obvious, that the laws are the rule of both, the common measure of the power of the Crown and of the obedience of the subject. [9]

For the Tories, Sir Simon Harcourt, a leading politician and lawyer, made the ablest defence of Sacheverell. Queen Anne, a strong Anglican, was in favour of leniency, and Sacheverell was sentenced only to have his sermon burnt in public and to be prevented from preaching for three years. The trial and its aftermath were attended by widespread popular riots, some with Jacobite overtones, and several of the Whig managers of the trial had to flee for their lives. Sacheverell became a popular hero and made a triumphal tour throughout England followed by vast adulatory crowds. [10] From the pulpit of Salisbury Cathedral on 5 November 1710 Burnet challenged Sacheverell and his followers and reaffirmed Revolution principles, concluding:

Thus I have deduced the grounds upon which the Revolution was carried on and established, which must be looked on as a continued usurpation to this day, if these principles are not true, all the oaths taken to support it are so many solemn perjuries, which are of no force unless built upon a sure foundation and the prayers we have been offering up relating to it are an impious profanation of the name of God. [11]

Under the influence of Robert Harley (who had fallen under Whig attack in 1708), the Queen dismissed Marlborough and Godolphin and Harley became Lord Treasurer. After the fall of Marlborough and Godolphin in 1710, a flood of Tory addresses in favour of peace poured in, denouncing Marlborough and his associates as 'the men that delight in war'. A well-informed contemporary wrote: 'it has always seemed to be very plain that the spirit of the gentry of the nation is Toryism, and that nothing but the influence of the Court has made it otherwise in any Parliament'. [12] He was right, and a landslide victory for the Tories followed at the general election of 1710. Like France, Britain was exhausted and nearing financial collapse. State borrowing to meet the cost of the war had reached such proportions that even Godolphin had been unable to find further credit. Harley, now Earl of Oxford, had two great achievements to his name. He restored public credit by skilful financial management and by making peace with France. Henry St John, Viscount

Bolingbroke wrote that the Tory ministers in 1710 'looked on the political principles, which had generally prevailed in our government from the revolution . . . to be obstructive of our true interest, to have mingled too much in the affairs of the continent, to tend to the impoverishment of our people'.[13]

The 1710 general election, in the course of which few of the usual kinds of government pressure and patronage were brought to bear, brought great Tory majorities in the Commons, but they were often foiled by the Whig majority in the Lords. Lord Poulett wrote in 1711: '[the] House of Lords prevails over the Queen's management with us and the strongest House of Commons that ever met'.[14] In 1712 Oxford (Robert Harley) had to get the Queen to create 12 new peers to get the peace through. Austria and Hanover rejected the peace terms outright.[15] The Tories were hampered by internal divisions. They were split between the Jacobites who would accept James III as a Roman Catholic, those who hoped James would conform to the Church of England, and the Hanoverian Tories who would not accept James even if he did conform. The Duke of Berwick, James II's natural son and Marlborough's nephew, one of the ablest generals in French service, kept in close touch with English affairs through the 2nd Duke of Ormonde, Marlborough's successor as Captain-General of the army. He thought there would have been a majority in favour of repealing the Act of Settlement. Oxford, however, persuaded the Jacobites, through instructions from James III, that the peace must be achieved first.[16] The proclamation of the peace saw the greatest scenes of joy in London since the Restoration of 1660. The territorial and commercial gains made at the Peace of Utrecht in 1713 were substantial: Britain acquired from France Newfoundland, the Hudson Bay territory, Acadia and St Kitts in the West Indies. France outwardly accepted the Hanoverian succession, while secretly negotiating with Oxford and Bolingbroke to try and achieve a Stuart restoration. The advantages of the Asiento contract with Spain, whereby Britain could supply negro slaves to the Spanish colonies, however, proved elusive. All in all, the gains were not proportionate to the immense costs of the war. The general election of 1713 brought another (slightly smaller) Tory majority in the Commons. The struggle for power between Oxford and Bolingbroke, who were in contact with the courts of Hanover and St-Germain simultaneously, and who seemed to think that they could remain in office after the Hanoverian succession, paralysed the Tory party and enabled the Whig minority to exploit the situation. In April 1714 Ormonde spoke to the Queen at long last about the succession and they 'both agreed to bestir themselves' on behalf of her half brother, James III.[17] When Queen Anne died suddenly in August 1714, the Barrier Treaties, which gave the Dutch the right to intervene in British domestic affairs to secure the Hanoverian succession, and were deeply resented by the Tories, were still in place and the Act of Settlement came into operation.

CONCLUSION

The Whig interpretation of history, propounded by Macaulay, argued that the Glorious Revolution had rescued Britain from tyranny and guided it towards political liberty, constitutional stability and economic progress. It laid the basis for parliamentary government and religious freedom, the best possible of revolutions. It led to the best possible form of government and avoided in the nineteenth century a bloody revolution on the model of the French Revolution of 1789 and the Terror of the 1790s. The Revolution was pictured as bloodless and consensual, with the role of the Tories in securing the transfer of the Crown to William and Mary and in the passing of the Act of Settlement greatly exaggerated. It was a Parliamentary revolution and the ruling elite, who sanctioned the Prince of Orange's triumph, were taken to be the true representative of the people. The new partnership between the Crown and Parliament released the financial resources which transformed Britain from a minor into a great power, with a unique imperial destiny.

The reassertion of the Whig interpretation by Trevelyan in *The English Revolution 1688–9* (1939) was challenged by Christopher Hill in *The English Revolution 1640* (1940). Karl Marx, earlier, saw the Revolution of 1688 as no more than a palace coup, and he criticised William of Orange as the instrument of the bourgeoisie and the agent of foreign policies based on commercial interests. Hill saw 1640, not 1688, as the start of the historical process leading to the French Revolution. The Levellers fascinated Marxist historians, with their radical demands for social change and that Parliament itself should be restricted by immutable fundamental laws and made more representative through frequent elections on a much wider franchise. The strong religious basis of the Levellers' views, however, was largely ignored or discounted in the Marxist interpretation.[1]

Historians today, led by Jonathan Israel and others, recognise the Revolution of 1688 as a successful invasion, accomplished with larger forces than those at James II's disposal, albeit one with little opposition from English people. It was motivated by strategic and diplomatic European considerations, not domestic English ones. The passivity of many Tories was due to their relying on William's assurances that he had no designs on the Crown and that, even if he became Regent, there would be no breach in the hereditary succession. The unpopularity of James II's policies provided the pretext for the invasion and a pretence of legitimacy to the ratification of a fait accompli, but it took a superior army to drive James away. The Prince of Orange had promised a free Parliament and, on the surface, the deliberations of the Convention of 1689 seem unrestricted by the Prince. The reality is that the debates in the 1689 Parliament were held in a London surrounded by Dutch troops, who were an army of occupation, and from which English troops had been sent away. With James gone, what alternative was there to coming to terms with William and agreeing to the transfer of the Crown to him and Mary as the only way of settling the government and avoiding the popular disorders feared by the governing classes? It was not a populist revolution. A good number of the men who came over with William of Orange had been involved in the Rye House Plot of 1683, the Argyll rebellion in Scotland in 1685 or the Monmouth rebellion of 1685 in England, and were Commonwealth men, regarded as republicans. One of them John Wildman, who became Postmaster-General in 1689, had been a leading Leveller. Yet the Commonwealth had little impact on the Revolution Settlement, which was conservationist.

The Glorious Revolution did not solve all the problems encountered by Stuart governments and its immediate effects in Britain were deeply divisive. It produced the longest-fought struggle over the royal succession in British history. Differences between the two political parties were fundamental and irreconcilable, not a mere question of ins and outs of office or different emphases over similar policies. The Tories, the 'Church party', were alarmed at the lack of commitment of William III to the Church of England, and the end of the close relationship established with the national Church by Charles I and Charles II. One of the reasons they took office was to defend the Church of England from within Parliament and the government. In the short term, with mixed ministries, it produced chaos and corruption in government. The suspending or dispensing powers of the monarch disappeared, but those of Parliament replaced them. Parliament repeatedly suspended the Habeas Corpus Act and the Treason Trials Act of 1696 for the attainders of Sir John Fenwick in 1696 and of Bishop Atterbury in 1723.

The years after 1715 did not witness a steady progress towards constitutional monarchy, as has sometimes been assumed. While Whig ministers paid lip service to Revolution principles, their actions belied them. On the contrary, several of the gains made after 1689 were reversed and there were calls for a free Parliament once again. George I, the Elector of Hanover, one of the most authoritarian and least flexible rulers in Europe, employed Whigs only. He never forgave the Tories for making peace with France and proscribed them from office both national and local after 1715, with the exception of the expensive and troublesome office of Sheriff, which Tories had to serve in all but election years when it was electorally advantageous. George II continued the proscription of the Tories after his accession in 1727. This produced a one-party state. The Septennial Act of 1716 prolonged the 1715 Parliament without holding an election and rendered general elections a seven-yearly instead of a three-yearly event. This strengthened the power of the executive over Parliament, as well as government and private patronage in the more easily manipulated boroughs. Had George I had his way, the 1715 Parliament, chosen after strong government pressure and at vast expense spent on bribery, would have lasted for the whole of his lifetime, without holding another election.[2] Other representative institutions were curbed. Convocation was not allowed to meet, so as to stifle the voice of the lower clergy.[3] Nor was the Cornish Parliament summoned, the Parliament of Tinners, which played an essential part in the economic as well as the political life of Cornwall.[4] The measures taken to bring the University of Cambridge under Whig control [5] dwarfed James II's efforts to bring the University of Oxford to obedience. Walpole had feared riots such as the Sacheverell riots in 1710 and the Jacobite riots in 1715 and thought the army was more reliable than the militia in controlling popular disturbances. MPs, he apparently thought, ought to be 'gentlemen of liberal fortune and tolerable education' rather than men 'bred to a trade and brought up in a shop'.[6] As the eighteenth century progressed, the right to vote in Parliamentary boroughs narrowed and the electorate became even less representative. Great aristocrats, who invested landed income in industry, were able to buy and control more and more venal boroughs with their increasing wealth. With ever more efficient Parliamentary management and an ever-increasing national debt, accountability to Parliament became less important. Commissions of Accounts no longer scrutinised public expenditure. George I came with a train of Germans, who took precedence in England until 1719 and had a German ministry in England as well as a British one.[7] The fact that George I and George II spent six months out of the year in Hanover did not mean increased powers for their English ministers. On the contrary, leading English ministers accompanied them to Hanover and the Lords of the Regency in England scrupulously referred decisions to the King in Hanover. British foreign policy was subordinated to the interests of Hanover, the lesser power, as it had been to the interests of the Dutch Netherlands in William's reign. All-Whig governments relying on Whig or venal boroughs won general elections easily and had ample funds provided by a pliant Parliament. This produced Parliamentary, but not political, stability. It has been assumed that the national debt, ever-growing since the Revolution, would be a vested interest too strong to allow for the Stuarts to be restored. This is not the case, as historians have not realised that Robert Harley, Earl of Oxford, who had turned to Jacobitism after 1715, persuaded James III to agree to assume responsibility for the national debt until the death of Queen Anne, thus assuring the financial interests of the fundholders.[8]

The resentments of the dispossessed and the excluded led to the Jacobite rebellions of 1715 and 1745. They failed mainly because they lacked the powerful foreign base and the massive use of professional troops which had made the Dutch invasion of 1688 succeed. The English militia were active against the Jacobites in some counties during the rebellion of 1715, but though they were purged of Tories, during the 1745 rebellion they refused to act against the rebels. Dutch troops were brought over to fight the Jacobites in 1715 and 1745. Hessian troops in British pay were brought over to England in 1745, but their commander, Prince Frederick of Hesse, refused to fight at Culloden because there were no provisions for a cartel (an agreement for the exchange of prisoners).[9] After 1689, 1715 and 1745 there was a massive Jacobite exile to the continent of Europe, as well as the Jacobites transported or emigrating to North America. Their numbers were greater than the Huguenot exile, and the loss to Britain was even greater than the loss of the Huguenots to France after 1685.

Tories were shocked when, after decades of Whig invective against France, the Whigs, in order to secure the Hanoverian succession, made Britain the closest ally of France between the years 1716 and 1730. When the Anglo-French alliance broke down in the 1730s, Marlborough's military triumphs were not repeated. In the War of the Austrian Succession (1740–48), Britain suffered successive defeats in Europe. George II's one success, the victory at Dettingen in 1743, was marred when he led the army wearing the yellow sash of Hanover and showed open preference to his Hanoverian officers, as William III had done to his Dutch officers during the Nine Years War. At the time the leaders of the Tory party in Parliament were actively negotiating with the French to restore the Stuarts. The years between the fall of Walpole in 1742 and the coming to power of Henry Pelham and his brother, the Duke of Newcastle in 1746 were years of political instability and a time fraught with peril for the Whig ruling elite.

Nor was Protestantism a unifying force. In England, there were deep antagonisms between the Church of England, the core of the Tory party (apart from Whig bishops) and the Dissenters, who were the mainstay of the Whigs in the constituencies. In Scotland the Presbyterians triumphed, leaving the Episcopalians little better off than the Roman Catholics. Wales, which had been simply annexed by Henry VIII and subjected to English law, had a different culture in which Jacobitism was a strong element, rather than forming a separate nation like the Scots. Religion there was not a unifying factor as it became predominantly Methodist in the eighteenth century. The Catholic majority in Ireland suffered most, with policies designed not so much to integrate them as to keep them in a state of permanent inferiority. George III prevented reforms giving Irish Catholics emancipation, which the Younger Pitt had promised as the price of accepting the Union of 1800 with England. Irish Presbyterians, too, were excluded from public life. Most of the troubles and conflicts so difficult to solve in Ireland today arose out of the Glorious Revolution.

On the positive side, state borrowing to finance the enormous costs of the Nine Years War had produced the financial revolution, which enabled Britain to become a world power in time. During the Seven Years War (1756–63) William Pitt the Elder, Earl of Chatham, made a major contribution to, in the words of Linda Colley's book *Britons*, 'forging the nation'. Chatham had earned the animosity of George II by his attacks on pro-Hanoverian policies in the past. In order to get and to keep in office, he now had to look after the interests of Hanover. Simultaneously, however, he adopted the blue-water policy so long advocated by the Tories. The pursuit of trade and sea power through successful war, together with military and naval victories over the French in 1759, the *Annus Mirabilis*, made him the most popular of all Whig ministers. His sending the Hessian and Hanoverian troops away from English soil and refusing to defend Britain with foreign mercenaries made him the darling of the City of London.[10] Gaining command of the seas over the French, Britain made vast acquisitions in India, Canada and elsewhere which shaped the British Empire. It gave great opportunities to Britons, particularly enterprising Scots. After the Napoleonic Wars Britain became the greatest power in Europe in the nineteenth century, as France had been in the seventeenth and eighteenth centuries, and the world's most powerful imperial power.

Parliament, which had played no part in bringing William of Orange over to England, shaped the Revolution Settlement and was the chief beneficiary of the Glorious Revolution. It secured annual sessions of Parliament for itself and, at first, tighter financial control. The Bill of Rights enshrined the rights and privileges of Parliament, but left the people as subjects with no basic rights as such. Parliament was an unrepresentative and self-interested body. It was flexible enough, however, to respond to the economic needs of England, usually expressed through petitions from constituencies, corporations and individuals. The royal prerogative was left virtually intact. The royal veto over Acts of Parliament was last exercised by Queen Anne in 1708, but the prerogative of the Hanoverian Georges remained great.

Montesquieu, the French philosopher, visited England from 1729 to 1731, when he was no less taken aback than William III had been by the ferocity of debates in the House of Commons. In *L'esprit des Lois* (1748) he argued that English liberty had been secured in the unwritten English constitution though the division of powers between the legislative, the executive, and the judiciary. He misunderstood a system in which ministers sat in the Commons or the Lords, and male heirs to the Crown and English judges sat in the Lords, while Welsh judges could sit in the Commons. It was not a tidy arrangement, but it had advantages. Montesquieu's views, however, were influential in shaping the American constitution. To Bolingbroke (Oxford's rival in the last years of Queen Anne's reign and a major eighteenth-century thinker), in his *Remarks on the History of England and A Dissertation upon Parties*, the King in Parliament after 1689 ensured not the separation of, but the balance of powers between, Crown, Lords and Commons. To avoid tyranny or anarchy each branch had to resist encroachments from the other two. He feared, however, that the erosion of the independence of Parliament by the executive during Walpole's prime-ministership might end by tipping the balance of power in favour of the Crown.[11] To George III the English constitution was the most perfect in the world and could not be altered in any way. George III opposed giving office to Irish Roman Catholics: 'no country can be governed where there is more than one established religion', and he was against Catholic emancipation: 'he must be the Protestant King of a Protestant country, or no King'. Similarly, he opposed granting toleration to non-Trinitarian Dissenters, as well as parliamentary reform.[12]

By the end of the eighteenth century, complacency disappeared. Radical Protestant Dissenters, such as Richard Price and Joseph Priestley (Unitarian Dissenting ministers), took up John Locke's contractual thesis once again, this time in the context of events in Revolutionary France. Price attempted to demonstrate the inadequacy of the Revolution Settlement:

> But the most important instance of the imperfect state in which the Revolution left our constitution is the INEQUALITY OF OUR REPRESENTATION. I think, indeed, this defect in our constitution so gross and so palpable, as to make it excellent chiefly in form and theory. You should remember that a representation in the legislature of a kingdom is the *basis* of constitutional liberty in it, and of all legitimate government, and that without it a government is nothing but an usurpation.[13]

Priestley, on his side, severely criticised the inadequacy of the Toleration Act of 1689 for leaving out Unitarians. Reformers, such as William Cobbett, exposed the absurdities and inequalities of the electoral system, while organisations such as the Society of Friends of Parliamentary Reform and the Union of Parliamentary Reform pressed their case in writing and in extraparliamentary agitation. The Government retaliated in 1795 by suspending the Habeas Corpus Act and passing statutes against seditious and treasonable practices.[14] Not until the defeat of Napoleon and Revolutionary France were Acts of Parliament passed to repeal penal laws against Unitarian Protestant Dissenters, to grant Catholic Emancipation and to begin the process of Parliamentary reform with the Great Reform Bill of 1832. It was in the nineteenth century, not in 1689, that real religious toleration, a representative Parliament (for males at least) and a constitutional monarchy came into being.

NOTES

I am obliged to Professor Jeremy Black for helpful suggestions and criticisms on the contents of this volume.

Introduction

1. G. B. Hill (ed.), *Boswell's Life of Johnson* (6 vols, Oxford, 1934–50), ii.341–2, 255 (I owe these references to the kindness of J. C. D. Clark).
2. J. C. D. Clark, *English Society 1688–1832* (Cambridge, 1985), p. 382 n.105.
3. *London Review of Books*, 24 November 1988.
4. Lois G. Schwoerer, 'Celebrating the Glorious Revolution, 1689–1989', *Albion*, XVIII (1990), 16–18. I owe a special debt to Lois Schwoerer for her generosity in giving me copies of her publications and for having had the benefit of conversations with her on several points made in this book.

1   The Restoration: Religious and Political Conflicts in the Reign of Charles II

1. See C. D. Chandaman, *The English Public Revenue 1660–85* (Oxford, 1975).
2. John Miller, *Charles II* (London, 1991), pp. 175, 241, 252.
3. John Miller, *Popery and Politics in England 1660–1688* (Cambridge, 1973), pp. 9–12.
4. A. Browning, *Thomas Osborne, Earl of Danby* (3 vols, Glasgow, 1951); B. D. Henning (ed.), *The House of Commons 1660–1690* (3 vols, London, 1983) (hereafter *HC*) iii.186–7.
5. Miller, *Charles II*, pp. 180, 236, 259. See K. H. D. Haley, *William of Orange and the English Opposition 1672–1674* (Oxford, 1953).
6. Sir John Dalrymple, *Memoirs of Great Britain and Ireland* (3 vols, London, 1790), i App. to chapter 4, pp. 382–6.
7. Almon, *Biographical, Literary and Political Anecdotes* (3 vols, London, 1797), iii.123–31.
8. Miller, *Charles II*, chapter 10.

2   The Popish Plot and the Exclusion Crisis, 1678–1681

1. Unless otherwise stated, references are to J. P. Kenyon, *The Popish Plot* (London, 1972), a feat of historical detection.
2. *HC* iii.250–1, 658–60, 377.
3. J. R. Jones, *The First Whigs* (London, 1961), pp. 53–4.
4. Tim Harris, *London Crowds in the Reign of Charles II: Politics and Propaganda from the Restoration until the Exclusion Crisis* (Cambridge, 1987), chapters 5, 6 and 7.
5. Miller, *Charles II*, p. 290.
6. Hugh Oulton, 'York in Edinburgh. James VII and the Patronage of Learning in Scotland 1679–1688', in J. Dwyer, B. A. Mason and A. Murdoch (eds), *New Perspectives on the Politics and Culture of Early Modern Scotland* (Glasgow, 1982), pp. 133–55; and 'From Thames to Tweed Departed: The Court of James, Duke of York in Scotland 1679–82', in Eveline Cruickshanks (ed.), *The Stuart Courts* (Stroud, forthcoming).
7. Ronald Hutton, *Charles II* (Oxford, 1989), p. 392.

3   The Tory Reaction, 1683–1686

1. Miller, *Charles II*, chapter 13.
2. *HC* i.314, iii.93.
3. Miller, *Charles II*, pp. 286, 360–5.
4. *HC* i.314.
5. Richard L. Greaves, *Secrets of the Kingdom: British Radicals from the Popish Plot to the Revolution of 1688–89* (Stanford, 1992), pp. 139–60. For Lord Russell's guilt, see Lois G. Schwoerer, 'The Trial of Lord William Russell 1683: Judicial Murder?', *Journal of Legal History*, Sept. 1988. Miller, *Charles II*, pp. 375–6. See also D. J. Milne, 'The Results of the Rye House Plot and their Influence on the Revolution of 1688', *Transactions of the Royal Historical Society* (hereafter *TRHS*), 5th ser. (1951), 81–108.
6. *HC* ii.469.
7. H. C. Foxcroft, *The Life and Letters of Sir George Savile, First Marquis of Halifax* (2 vols, London, 1898), i.425.

4   James II's Reign, Monmouth's Rebellion, Toleration for All, and the Anglican Backlash

1. J. R. Jones (ed.), *Liberty Secured? Britain Before and After 1688* (Stanford, CT, 1992), p. 15.
2. See D. Chandler, *Sedgmoor* (London, 1985).
3. Eveline Cruickshanks, David Hayton and Clyve Jones, 'Divisions in the House of Lords on the Transfer of the Crown and other Issues, 1689–94: Ten New Lists', *Bulletin of the Institute of Historical Research* (hereafter *BIHR*), LIII (1980), 65–8.
4. Robert Beddard, *A Kingdom without a King* (Oxford, 1988), pp. 14–15.
5. Jones, *Liberty*, p. 21.

6. See Oulton, 'York in Edinburgh'.
7. J. R. Jones, *The Revolution of 1688 in England* (London, 1972), p. 101.
8. Edward Corp, 'James II and Toleration: The Years in Exile at Saint-Germain-en-Laye', *Royal Stuart Papers*, LI (London, 1997).
9. Jones, *Liberty*, p. 22.
10. Eveline Cruickshanks, 'Religion and Royal Succession', in Clyve Jones (ed.), *Britain in the First Age of Party 1680–1750* (London, 1967), p. 23.
11. Sir George Duckett, *Penal Laws and Test Act* (2 vols, London, 1882–83).
12. John Miller, 'James II and Toleration', in Eveline Cruickshanks (ed.), *By Force or By Default: The Revolution of 1688–89* (Edinburgh, 1989), p. 8.
13. Beddard, *Kingdom*, p. 14.
14. Howard Nenner, 'Liberty, Law and Property: The Constitution in Retrospect from 1689', in Jones, *Liberty*, pp. 109–10.
15. Mark Goldie, 'The Political Thought of the Anglican Revolution', in Robert Beddard, *The Revolutions of 1688. The Andrew Browning Lectures 1988* (Oxford, 1991), pp. 116, 123.
16. Jonathan Israel, *The Anglo-Dutch Moment: Essays on the Glorious Revolution and its World Impact* (Cambridge, 1991), p. 12.
17. J. P. Kenyon, *Robert Spencer, Earl of Sunderland 1641–1702* (London, 1958), p. 197.
18. Eveline Cruickshanks, 'The Revolution in the Localities' in Cruickshanks, *By Force*, p. 39.
19. For Ashton see Edward Corp and Jacqueline Sanson (eds), *La Cour des Stuarts à Saint-Germain-en-Laye au temps de Louis XIV* (exhibition catalogue, Paris, 1992), p. 78.
20. Goldie, in Beddard, *Revolutions*, pp. 102, 118.
21. Kenyon, *Sunderland*, p. 199.
22. See R. Thomas, 'The Seven Bishops and their Petition', *Journal of Ecclesiastical History*, XI (1966), 56–70; G. V. Bennett, 'The Seven Bishops: a Reconsideration', in D. Baker (ed.), *Religious Motivation, Studies in Church History*, XV (London, 1978), pp. 267–87.
23. Nenner, in Jones, *Liberty*, pp. 113–15.
24. Eveline Cruickshanks, 'Attempts to Restore the Stuarts, 1689–96', in Eveline Cruickshanks and Edward Corp (eds), *The Stuart Court in Exile and the Jacobites* (London, 1995), pp. 1–13.
25. Tim Harris, 'London Crowds and the Revolution of 1688', in Cruickshanks, *By Force*, pp. 51, 55.
26. Eveline Cruickshanks, 'The Revolution and the Localities: Examples of Loyalty to James II', in Jones, *Age of Party*, p. 22.
27. Goldie, in Beddard, *Revolutions*, p. 109.

5 The International Coalition against France and the Dutch Invasion

1. Israel, *Anglo-Dutch Moment*, p. 12.
2. John Childs, *The Army, James II and the Glorious Revolution* (Manchester, 1980), pp. 138–41, 169–98. See also W. A. Speck, 'The Orangist Conspiracy against James II', *Historical Journal* (hereafter *HJ*), XXX (1987), 453–62.

3. Jeremy Black, 'The Revolution and the Development of English Foreign Policy', in Cruickshanks, *By Force*, p. 143.
4. John Stoye, 'Europe and the Revolution of 1688', in Beddard, *Revolutions*, p. 205.
5. Geoffrey Symcox, 'Louis XIV and the Outbreak of the Nine Years War', in Ragnhild Hatton (ed.), *Louis XIV and Europe* (London, 1976), pp. 179–92, 205; Paul Sonino, 'The Origins of Louis XIV's Wars', in Jeremy Black (ed.), *The Origin of War in Early Modern Europe* (Edinburgh, 1987), pp. 124–9.
6. Black, in Cruickshanks, *By Force*, p. 150.
7. Dale Hoak, 'The Anglo-Dutch Revolution of 1688–89', in Dale Hoak and Mordechai Feingold (eds), *The World of William and Mary: Anglo-Dutch Perspectives on the Revolution of 1688–89* (Stanford, CT, 1996), pp. 17–18.
8. David Davies, 'James II, William of Orange and the Admirals', in Cruickshanks, *By Force*, pp. 82–108.
9. Hoak, 'Anglo-Dutch Revolution', p. 17.
10. Cruickshanks, *By Force*, p. 29; Surrey Record Office, Guildford, Onslow Ms. 173/338/3.
11. Childs, *Army*, p. 21.
12. Israel, *Anglo-Dutch Moment*, p. 13.
13. Lois G. Schwoerer, 'Liberty of the Press and Public Opinion 1660–1695', in Jones, *Liberty*, pp. 222–3.
14. William Cobbett, *The Parliamentary History of England* (36 vols, London, 1806–20), vol. 10. For the text of William's Declarations, see Sir James Mackintosh, *History of the Revolution* (Philadelphia, PA, 1825), pp. 708–20.
15. Howard Nenner, *The Right to be King: The Succession to the Crown of England, 1603–1714* (London, 1995), p. 158.
16. Cruickshanks, *By Force*, pp. 17, 28–9, 31–3, 36–7.
17. See D. H. Hosford, *Nottingham, Nobles and the North* (Hamden, CT, 1976) and J. P. Kenyon, *The Nobility in the Revolution of 1688* (Hull, 1963).
18. W. A. Speck, *Reluctant Revolutionaries: Englishmen and the Revolution of 1688* (Oxford, 1988), p. 7.
19. Beddard, *Kingdom*, p. 23.
20. Childs, *Army*, p. 142.
21. Hoak, 'Anglo-Dutch Revolution', p. 18.
22. Beddard, *Kingdom*, pp. 23–5.
23. S. W. Singer (ed.), *The Correspondence of Henry Hyde, Earl of Clarendon* (hereafter *Clarendon Corresp.*) (2 vols, London, 1828), ii.206–7; J. S. Clarke, *The Life of James II* (2 vols, London, 1816), ii.222–4.
24. Jones, *Revolution*, p. 295.
25. Cruickshanks, *By Force*, pp. 31–2.
26. Beddard, *Kingdom*, pp. 25–8.
27. Jones, *Liberty*, p. 310.
28. Beddard, *Kingdom*, pp. 29–34.
29. Cruickshanks, *By Force*, p. 32.
30. Beddard, *Kingdom*, pp. 38–46, 50–1, 55, 57.
31. Beddard, *Revolutions*, p. 70. Dr Beddard is quite right in correcting statements in *HC* i.310, 314 asserting that the City of London did not take an active part in the Revolution, and that there was little disorder there in 1688.

These statements were inserted in my London article (in B. D. Henning (ed.), *The House of Command 1660–90* for the History of Parliament), when these volumes were prepared for publication without my knowledge or consent, and I welcome this opportunity to correct them.

32. Beddard, *Kingdom*, p. 60.
33. Israel, *Anglo-Dutch Moment*, pp. 1–2.
34. For James's own account of these events see Clarke, *James II*, ii.273–5 and British Library Add. Ms. 29252 f. 35. Beddard, *Kingdom*, p. 62.
35. David Ogg, *England in the Reigns of James II and William III* (Oxford, 1955), p. 223.
36. Beddard, *Kingdom*, p. 62.
37. G. S. de Krey, *The Fractured Society. The Politics of London in the First Age of Party, 1688–1715* (Oxford, 1985), p. 20.
38. Beddard, *Kingdom*, p. 65.
39. Childs, *Army*, p. 205.

6 The 1689 Convention, the Settlement of the Crown and the Bill of Rights

1. Nenner, *Right*, p. 155.
2. *Clarendon Corresp.*, ii.234–5, 238, 244, 251–3.
3. Speck, *Reluctant*, p. 91.
4. *HC* ii.487.
5. I noticed this while searching, on behalf of the History of Parliament, the original returns, which are kept in sacks at the Public Record Office.
6. Historical Manuscripts Commission (hereafter *HMC*) *Diary of Viscount Percival, afterwards 1st Earl of Egmont* (3 vols, London, 1920–23), iii.226.
7. Nenner, *Right*, chapter 7 and pp. 250–1.
8. J. G. A. Pocock, 'The Significance of 1688: Some Reflections on Whig History', in Beddard, *Revolutions*, p. 276.
9. Lois G. Schwoerer, 'The Right to Resist: Whig Resistance Theory, 1688–1694', in Nicholas Phillipson and Quentin Skinner (eds), *Political Discourse in Early Modern Britain* (Cambridge, 1995), pp. 242–4; Gordon G. Schochet, 'John Locke and Religious Toleration', in Lois G. Schwoerer (ed.), *The Revolution of 1688–1689: Changing Perspectives* (Cambridge, 1992), pp. 147–68. See also Mark Goldie, 'The Roots of True Whiggism, 1688–1694', *History of Political Thought*, I (1980), 195–236.
10. Clark, *English Society*, pp. 273, 280.
11. Cruickshanks, in Jones, *Age of Party*, p. 25.
12. Speck, *Reluctant*, pp. 96, 97–8.
13. *HC* ii.323, iii.43.
14. Anchitel Grey, *Debates in the House of Commons from the Year 1667 to the Year 1694* (10 vols, London, 1763), ix.26.
15. Cobbett, *Parliamentary History*, v. 39, 50, 98; B. W. Hill, *The Growth of Parliamentary Parties 1689–1742* (London, 1976), p. 33.
16. J. P. Kenyon, *Revolution Principles: The Politics of Party 1689–1720* (Cambridge, 1977), p. 8.

17. Speck, *Reluctant*, pp. 99–102.
18. de Krey, *Fractured Society*, p. 213.
19. Speck, *Reluctant*, p. 103; *HC* iii.585; Cruickshanks, Hayton and Jones, 'Divisions', p. 64; Eveline Cruickshanks, John Ferris and David Hayton, 'The House of Commons Vote on the Transfer of the Crown, 5 February 1689', *BIHR*, LII (1979), 37–47.
20. Gilbert Burnet, *History of his Own Time* (6 vols, Oxford, 1933), iii.395.
21. Paul Monod, 'Jacobitism and Country Principles in the Reign of William III', *HJ*, XXX (1987), 292–95; A. Browning (ed.), *The Memoirs of Sir John Reresby* (hereafter *Reresby Memoirs*) (Glasgow, 1936), p. 553.
22. Jones, *Liberty*, pp. 30, 31.
23. Schwoerer, 'Celebrating', 3.
24. Cruickshanks, Hayton and Jones, 'Divisions', p. 61.
25. Nenner, *Right*, p. 165.
26. *Dictionary of National Biography*, entry for Gilbert Burnet.
27. Lois G. Schwoerer, *The Declaration of Rights 1689* (Baltimore, MD, 1981) and 'The English Bill of Rights 1689', in Stephen F. Englehart and John Allphin Moore Jun. (eds), *A Perspective on Liberty – Three Beginnings: Revolution, Rights and the Liberal State. Comparative Perspectives on the English, American and French Revolutions* (Washington, DC, 1994); R. J. Frankle, 'The Formulation of the Declaration of Rights' *HJ*, XVII (1974), 265–79.
28. *Reresby Memoirs*, pp. 546–7, 554.
29. Robert Bucholz, *The Augustan Court; Queen Anne and the Decline of Court Culture* (Stanford, CT, 1993), pp. 28–35.
30. Greaves, *Secrets of the Kingdom*, p. 350. Childs, *Army*, p. 146.
31. Stephen N. Swicker, 'Representing the Revolution: Politics and High Culture in 1688', in Cruickshanks, *By Force*, pp. 109–34.
32. Foxcroft, *Halifax*, Spencer House 'Journals', ii.200–52.
33. Hill, *Growth*, p. 37.
34. Jones, *Revolution*, p. 321.
35. Kenyon, *Revolution Principles*, pp. 20, 50.
36. *Reresby Memoirs*, p. 572.
37. *The Remains of Dennis Granville* (Surtees Society, 1860, XXXVII), 45–7.
38. *HC* iii.49.
39. Cruickshanks, Hayton and Jones, 'Divisions', pp. 65–7.
40. Foxcroft, *Halifax*, ii.95.
41. *HC* ii.44.
42. Hill, *Growth*, pp. 43–4.
43. Foxcroft, *Halifax*, ii.203–47.

7 Scotland and the Revolution

1. Ian B. Cowan, 'The Reluctant Revolutionaries: Scotland in 1688', in Cruickshanks, *By Force*, p. 68.
2. Bruce P. Lenman, 'The Scottish Nobility and the Revolution of 1688–1690', in Beddard, *Revolutions*, p. 145; W. Ferguson, *Scotland 1689 to the Present* (4 vols, Edinburgh, 1968), i. chapters 1 and 2.

3. Keith M. Brown, *Kingdom or Province? Scotland and the Regal Union 1603–1715* (London, 1992), pp. 17, 163, 164, 167, 169 and Oulton, 'York in Edinburgh'.
4. Cowan, in Cruickshanks, *By Force*, pp. 69–70.
5. Ian B. Cowan, 'Church and State Reformed? The Revolution of 1688–89 in Scotland', in Israel, *Anglo-Dutch Moment*, pp. 163–4.
6. Cowan, in Cruickshanks, *By Force*, p. 77.
7. P. A. Hopkins, 'Sir James Montgomerie of Skermorlie', in Cruickshanks and Corp, *Stuart Court in Exile*, pp. 44–5.
8. Cowan, in Israel, *Anglo-Dutch Moment*, pp. 166–7, 169; Cruickshanks, *By Force*, p. 77.
9. Cowan, in Israel, *Anglo-Dutch Moment*, pp. 169, 172. Hopkins, in Cruickshanks and Corp, *Stuart Court in Exile*, pp. 43–5.
10. Cowan, in Israel, *Anglo-Dutch Moment*, pp. 173–4.
11. Lenman, in Beddard, *Revolutions*, p. 158.
12. Cowan, in Israel, *Anglo-Dutch Moment*, pp. 174, 177, 180–2. Brown, *Kingdom or Province?*, p. 178.
13. Brown, *Kingdom or Province?*, p. 17.
14. See B. Lenman and J. Gibson, *The Jacobite Threat* (Edinburgh, 1980); P. Hopkins, *Glencoe and the Highland War* (Edinburgh, 1980).
15. G. P. R. James (ed.), *Letters Illustrative of the Reign of William III from 1696 to 1708. Addressed by the Duke of Shrewsbury to James Vernon* (3 vols, London, 1841), ii.408.
16. G. H. Healey (ed.), *Letters of Daniel Defoe* (Oxford, 1955), pp. 236–8, 243–4.
17. Brown, *Kingdom or Province?*, p. 72; Daniel Szechi (ed.), *Letters of George Lockhart of Carnwarth 1698–1732* (Edinburgh, 1989), pp. 1–116; P. W. J. Riley, *The Union of England and Scotland* (Manchester, 1978).
18. J. S. Gibson, *Playing the Scottish Card: The Franco-Jacobite Invasion of 1708* (Edinburgh, 1988).
19. Bruce Lenman, 'The Scottish Episcopal Clergy and the Ideology of Jacobitism', in Eveline Cruickshanks (ed.), *Ideology and Conspiracy: Aspects of Jacobitism 1689–1759* (Edinburgh, 1982), pp. 36–48; Murray G. H. Pittock, *The Invention of Scotland. The Stuart Myth and the Scottish Identity 1638 to the Present* (London, 1991) and *The Myth of the Jacobite Clans* (Edinburgh, 1995); Claude Nordmann, 'Les Jacobites écossais en France au XVIIIᵉ Siècle', in M. S. Plaisant (ed.), *Regards sur l'Écosse* (Université de Lille II, 1977), pp. 81–100.
20. Eveline Cruickshanks and Howard Erskine-Hill, *The Atterbury Plot* (Macmillan, forthcoming).

8 Ireland and the Revolution

1. Eveline Cruickshanks, 'The Political Career of the Third Earl of Burlington', in Toby Barnard and Jane Clark (eds), *Lord Burlington, Architecture, Art and Life* (London, 1995), p. 203.
2. D. W. Hayton, 'The Williamite Revolution in Ireland, 1688–91', in Israel, *Anglo-Dutch Moment*, pp. 185–91.
3. Karl S. Bottigheimer, 'The Glorious Revolution and Ireland', in Schwoerer, *Revolution*, p. 238.

4. Hayton, in Israel, *Anglo-Dutch Moment*, pp. 192, 195, 199.
5. Clarke, *James II*, ii.361–2.
6. Hayton, in Israel, *Anglo-Dutch Moment*, p. 195; Pierre Joannon, 'Jacques II et l'expédition d'Irlande', in Edward Corp (ed.), *L'Autre Exil. Les Jacobites en France au début du XVIIIe Siècle* (Presses du Languedoc, 1993), pp. 23–42.
7. Paper given by James Macguire in the Institute of Historical Research, University of London on his work in progress on the 1689 Irish Parliament, and J. S. Simms, *The Jacobite Parliament of 1689* (Dundalk, 1966).
8. Patrick Kelly, 'Ireland and the Glorious Revolution: From Kingdom to Colony', in Beddard, *Revolutions*, p. 170.
9. Macguire's paper (see n.7) and Hayton, in Israel, *Anglo-Dutch Moment*, pp. 195–7, 198.
10. Goldie, in Beddard, *Revolutions*, p. 128.
11. Hayton, in Israel, *Anglo-Dutch Moment*, pp. 198–9.
12. Peter Nockles, 'The Church of Ireland 1822–1869' *HJ*, XII (1998), 458.
13. Hayton, in Israel, *Anglo-Dutch Moment*, p. 203.
14. J. G. Simms, *Jacobite Ireland, 1685–1691* (London, 1969), pp. 155–7.
15. Hayton, in Israel, *Anglo-Dutch Moment*, pp. 207, 209–10; Kelly, in Beddard, *Revolutions*, pp. 163–4, 185.
16. Hayton, in Israel, *Anglo-Dutch Moment*, pp. 209–10. Bottigheimer, in Schwoerer, *Revolution*, pp. 234–43.
17. Louis Cullen, 'Catholics under the Penal Laws', *Eighteenth Century Ireland* (Dublin, 1986), pp. 23–36.
18. Kelly, in Beddard, *Revolutions*, pp. 164, 189.
19. Hayton, in Israel, *Anglo-Dutch Moment*, p. 211. This narrow, insular view is contradicted by Professor Brendan Ó Buchella. It is very much hoped Professor Ó Buchella will publish an English translation of his massive work on Irish Jacobitism recently published in Irish.
20. J. G. Simms, *Williamite Confiscation 1690–1703* (London, 1956), App. B.
21. Nathalie Genet-Rouffiac, 'Jacobites in Paris and Saint-Germain-en-Laye', in Cruickshanks and Corp, *Stuart Court in Exile*, pp. 15–21, and 'Un Episode de la Présence Britannique en France. Les Jacobites à Paris et Saint-Germain-en-Laye 1688–1714' (thesis, Ecole des Chartres, 1991), pp. 331–78 and chapter 8. I am grateful to Nathalie Genet-Rouffiac for permission to cite her two theses.
22. Eveline Cruickshanks, 'The 2nd Duke of Ormonde and the Atterbury Plot', in Toby and Jane Barnard Fenlon (eds), *The Dukes of Ormonde* (Woodbridge, forthcoming).
23. Nordmann, 'Les Jacobites écossais' (including the Irish).
24. Ex. inf. Eammon Ó Ciardha.

9 The War with France, Jacobite Opposition, Parliament and the Financial Settlement

1 Hill, *Growth*, pp. 47, 54–7; *Commons Journal*, XIV, 433–4.
2. Eveline Cruickshanks, 'Attempts to Restore the Stuarts, 1689–96', in Cruickshanks and Corp, *Stuart Court in Exile*, pp. 2–13.

3. Burnet, *History*, iv.5–6.
4. See Henry Horwitz, *Revolution Politicks. The Career of Daniel Finch, Second Earl of Nottingham 1647–1730* (Cambridge, 1968).
5. Browning, *Danby*, iii.App. 173–87.
6. Clark, *English Society*, p. 20. W. A. Speck, 'The Electorate in the First Age of Party', in Jones, *Age of Party*, pp. 46–60. See also W. A. Speck, *Tory and Whig. The Struggle in the Constituencies, 1701–1715* (London, 1970).
7. Paul Langford, *A Polite and Commercial People. England 1727–1783* (Oxford, 1989), pp. 711–12.
8. Bernard Cottret, *Cromwell* (Paris, 1992), pp. 415, 442–5.
9. Ogg, *England*, p. 349.
10. Genet-Rouffiac, *'Un Episode'*, pp. 385, 400.
11. See P. A. Hopkins, 'Aspects of the Jacobite Conspiracy in England in the Reign of William III' (Ph.D. thesis, University of Cambridge, 1981).
12. John Brewer, *The Sinews of Power, War, Money and the English State 1688–1783* (London, 1989), p. 50.
13. Ogg, *England*, pp. 352–6; J. Erhrman, *The Navy in the War of William III* (Cambridge, 1953), chapter 10.
14. Genet-Rouffiac, in Cruickshanks and Corp, *Stuart Court in Exile*, pp. 5, 29.
15. Cruickshanks, in Cruickshanks and Corp, *Stuart Court in Exile*, pp. 2–13.
16. Clarke, *James II*, ii.522. For the descent, see John Childs, *The British Army of William III 1689–1702* (Manchester, 1987), pp. 218–37.
17. Nathalie Genet-Rouffiac, 'La Première Génération de l'Exil Jacobite à Paris et à Saint-Germain-en-Laye 1688–1715' (doctoral thesis, Ecole Pratique des Hautes Etudes, 1995), p. 399.
18. Ogg, *England*, pp. 393–5.
19. Robert Molesworth, *An Account of the State of Denmark as it was in the year 1692* (London, 1694).
20. For Louis's army see John Lynn, *Giant of the Grand Siècle: The French Army 1610–1715* (Cambridge, 1997).
21. Ogg, *England*, chapter 13. John Childs, *The Nine Years War and the British Army 1688–1697* (Manchester, 1991), chapters 7 and 8.

10   The Anger of Parliament, the Country Party, Courtly Reformation and the Reform of Manners

1 Childs, *British Army of William III*, p. 324.
2. D. Rubini, *Court and Country 1688–1702* (London, 1968); R. Walcott, *English Politics in the Early Eighteenth Century* (Oxford, 1956).
3. Monod, 'Jacobitism'.
4. Hill, *Growth*, pp. 52–3; J. A. Downie, 'The Commission of Public Accounts and the Formation of the Country Party', *English Historical Review* (hereafter *EHR*), XCI (1976), 33–5.
5. *HC* ii.358.
6. Hill, *Growth*, pp. 54–5.

7. Anchitell Grey, *Debates of the House of Commons from the year 1667 to the year 1694*, 10 vols (London, 1763), x.341, 332; Ogg, *England*, p. 390.
8. Bath Mss. at Longleat, Thynne Papers XXIV ff. 207-8.
9. Draft biography for Eveline Cruickshanks, Stuart Hanley and David Hayton (eds), *The House of Commons 1690-1715* (Cambridge, forthcoming).
10. Hill, *Growth*, p. 55.
11. Geoffrey Holmes, *British Politics in the Age of Anne* (London, 1967), p. 67.
12. Israel, *Anglo-Dutch Moment*, p. 42.
13. Tony Claydon, *William III and the Godly Revolution* (Cambridge, 1996), p. 3. For the doctrine of divine right by providence see Clark, *English Society*.
14. Howard Erskine-Hill, 'Literature and the Jacobite Cause. Was There a Rhetoric of Jacobitism?', in Cruickshanks, *Ideology and Conspiracy*, p. 50.
15. Claydon, *William III*, pp. 18, 39, 49, 65, 83, 112, 131, 143.
16. Kenyon, *Revolution Principles*, pp. 162-3.
17. Tina Isaacs, 'The Anglican Hierarchy and the Reformation of Manners', *Journal of Ecclesiastical History*, XXXIII (1982), 391-411; R. Shoemaker, 'Reforming the City: The Reformation of Manners Campaign in London 1690-1738', in Lee Davison, Tim Hitchcock, Tim Kearns and Robert Shoemaker (eds), *Stilling the Grumbling Hive: The Response to Social and Economic Problems in England* (London, 1992), pp. 99-120; David Hayton, 'Moral Reform and Country Politics in the Late Seventeenth Century House of Commons', *Past and Present*, CXXVIII (1992), 48-91; Craig Rose, 'Providence, Protestant Union and Godly Reformation in the 1690s', *TRHS*, 6th ser. (1993), 151-70.
18. Cruickshanks, Hayton and Jones, 'Divisions', pp. 69-73.
19. Hill, *Growth*, pp. 56-7, 59.

11 The Whig Junto, the Foundation of the Bank of England and the Financial Revolution

1. J. P. Kenyon, 'The Earl of Sunderland and the King's Administration, 1693-1695', *EHR*, LXXI (1956), p. 581.
2. Hill, *Growth*, p. 69.
3. Burnet, *History*, iv. 295.
4. Hill, *Growth*, p. 75.
5. Brewer, *Sinews of Power*, chapter 4.
6. Ogg, *England*, chapter 14. Sir John Clapham, *The Bank of England* (London, 1944).
7. P. G. M. Dickson, *The Financial Revolution in England* (London, 1967).
8. Hill, *Growth*, p. 60.
9. M. J. Braddick, *Parliamentary Taxation in 17th Century England* (Royal Historical Society, Woodbridge, 1994), pp. 168-203.
10. Brewer, *Sinews of Power*, pp. 40, 91, 101-14, 135, 211-14.
11. Dickson, *Financial Revolution*, pp. 265, 300, 392.
12. de Krey, *Fractured Society*, p. 44.

13. Henry Horwitz, 'Party in a Civic Context: London from the Exclusion Crisis to the Fall of Walpole', in Jones, *Age of Party*, pp. 173–84.
14. Cruickshanks, in Jones, *Age of Party*, p. 26.
15. Ogg, *England*, pp. 422–5.

12 The Fenwick Plot and the Assassination Plot of 1696, the Peace of Ryswick, Moves to Restore the Stuarts

1. Paul Monod, 'The Jacobite Press and English Censorship 1689–95', in Cruickshanks and Corp, *Stuart Court in Exile*, pp. 125–42; Schwoerer, in Jones, *Liberty*, pp. 199–230.
2. Kenyon, *Revolution Principles*, p. 38.
3. *HC* ii.370.
4. Cruickshanks, in Cruickshanks and Corp, *Stuart Court in Exile*, pp. 6–12. Robert J. Frankle, 'Parliament's Right to do Wrong. The Parliamentary Attainder against Sir John Fenwick, 1696', *Parliamentary History*, IV (1985), 71–85.
5. Henry Horwitz, *Parliament, Policy and Politics in the Reign of William III* (Manchester, 1977), p. 175.
6. Genet-Rouffiac, 'Première Génération', p. 136; G. H. Jones, *Charles Middleton* (Chicago, 1967), p. 168.
7. Corp and Sanson, *La Cour des Stuarts*, and Cruickshanks and Corp, *Stuart Court in Exile*, introduction.
8. Ogg, *England*, p. 440.
9. *HC* ii.663.
10. D. W. Hayton (ed.), *The Parliamentary Diary of Sir Richard Cocks 1698–1702* (Oxford, 1997).
11. H. T. Dickinson, 'The Precursors of Political Radicalism in Augustan Britain', in Jones, *Age of Party*, pp. 63–71, and *Liberty and Property. Political Ideology in Eighteenth Century Britain* (London, 1977), chapters 2 and 4.
12. Hill, *Growth*, pp. 79–80.
13. Ogg, *England*, pp. 440–1.
14. Lois G. Schwoerer, *No Standing Armies! The Anti-Army Ideology in Seventeenth Century England* (Baltimore, MD, 1974).
15. David Hayton, 'The "Country" Interest and the Party System, 1689–c.1720', in Clyve Jones (ed.), *Party and Management of Parliament 1660–1784* (Leicester, 1984), pp. 37–85.

13 The Spanish Succession and the Act of Settlement

1. Ogg, *England*, p. 461. Hatton, *Louis XIV*, p. 298.
2. Genet-Rouffiac, 'Première Génération', p. 136; T. Aronson, *Kings over the Water* (London, 1979), pp. 64–5.
3. Cruickshanks, in Jones, *Age of Party*, p. 30.
4. *Vernon–Shrewsbury Corresp.*, iii.137–8 (see ch.7, n.15).

5. Hill, *Growth*, pp. 73, 86.
6. Ogg, *England*, p. 459. Cruickshanks, in Jones, *Age of Party*, p. 30.
7. British Library Add. Mss. 30,000E ff. 67–8.
8. Hill, *Growth*, p. 86–7.
9. John Campbell, *Lives of the Lords Chancellor*, 8 vols (London, 1845–69), iv.348.
10. Hill, *Growth*, p. 87.
11. Ogg, *England*, chapter 16.
12. Bruno Neveu, 'A Contribution to an Inventory of Jacobite Sources', in Cruickshanks, *Ideology and Conspiracy*, pp. 144–5.
13. E. H. Ellis (ed.), *Poems on Affairs of State 1697–1714* (New Haven, CT, 1970), iv.362–3. Attempts to get these works of art returned to Windsor failed.

14 The War of the Spanish Succession, the Death of Queen Anne and the Hanoverian Succession

1. E. Greg, *Queen Anne* (London, 1980), p. 122.
2. This point was first made to me by the late Geoffrey Holmes.
3. See Frances Harris, *A Passion for Government. The Life of Sarah, Duchess of Marlborough* (Oxford, 1991).
4. D. W. Jones, 'Defending the Revolution', in Hoak, *Anglo-Dutch Revolution*, p. 60.
5. Henry Roseveare, *The Treasury 1660–1870. The Foundations of Control* (London, 1973), pp. 142–4.
6. Cobbett, *Parliamentary History*, vii.577–8.
7. Geoffrey Holmes, *The Trial of Doctor Sacheverell* (London, 1973), pp. 222–55.
8. Cruickshanks, in Jones, *Age of Party*, p. 33.
9. Yale University, Beinecke Library, Osborn Coll. box 21 no. 22 f. 9, 'Account of the trial of Dr. Sacheverell'.
10. Holmes, *Trial of Doctor Sacheverell*, ch. 10.
11. Kenyon, *Revolution Principles*, p. 163.
12. Holmes, *British Politics*, p. 248.
13. *Letter to Sir William Wyndham* (London, 1717).
14. Clyve Jones, 'The House of Lords and the Growth of Parliamentary Stability', in Jones, *Age of Party*, p. 85.
15. Jeremy Black, *Just and Necessary Enemies; Anglo-French Relations in the Eighteenth Century* (London, 1986), p. 3.
16. See Daniel Szechi, *Jacobitism and Tory Politics 1710–1714* (Edinburgh, 1984), chapters 4 and 5.
17. HMC, Stuart Papers, i.517. E. Greg, in 'Was Queen Anne a Jacobite?', *History*, LVII (1972), 358–75, missed this evidence. Greg's contention lacks hard evidence (Hill, *Growth*, p. 144), and the destruction of Queen Anne's papers by George I does not suggest they were filled with enthusiasm for the Hanoverian succession.

Conclusion

1   K. Marx and F. Engels, *On Britain* (London, 1962), pp. 345, 347–8; C. Hill, 'A
    Bourgeois Revolution', in J. G. A. Pocock (ed.), *Three British Revolutions:
    1641, 1688–9, 1776* (Princeton, NJ, 1980).

2   J. C. D. Clark, *Revolution and Rebellion. State and Society in England in the Seventeenth and Eighteenth Centuries* (Cambridge, 1986), p. 75.

3   Paul Langford, 'Convocation and the Tory Clergy 1717–61', in Eveline
    Cruickshanks and Jeremy Black (eds), *The Jacobite Challenge* (Edinburgh,
    1988), pp. 107–22.

4   Eveline Cruickshanks, 'The Convocation of the Stannaries of Cornwall: The
    Parliament of Tinners 1703–1752', *Parliaments, Estates and Representation*, VI
    (1986), 59–67.

5   Romney Sedgwick (ed.), *The House of Commons 1715–1754* (2 vols, London,
    1970), i.201–2.

6   Kenyon, *Revolution Principles*, p. 206.

7   Clark, *Revolution and Rebellion*, p. 75.

8   Cruickshanks, in Jones, *Age of Party*, p. 3.

9   Eveline Cruickshanks, *Political Untouchables; The Tories and the '45* (London,
    1979), pp. 36–65; Jeremy Black, *Culloden and the '45'* (Stroud, 1990),
    pp. 155–8.

10 Marie Peters, *Pitt and Popularity. The Patriot Minister and London Opinion during the Seven Years War* (Oxford, 1980).

11 *The Works of Lord Bolingbroke* (4 vols, London, 1967), i.296–7, ii.15; H. T.
    Dickinson, *Bolingbroke* (London, 1970), pp. 202–6.

12 Ian Christie, *Wars and Revolution: Britain 1760–1815* (London, 1982),
    pp. 254, 279–80; Clark, *English Society*, p. 335.

13 Clark, *English Society*, p. 332.

14 Christie, *Wars and Revolution*, pp. 252, 305; Clark, *English Society*, pp. 330–7.

SELECT BIBLIOGRAPHY OF PRINTED WORKS (EXCLUDING THOSE CITED IN THE NOTES)

Ashcraft, Richard, *Revolution Politics and Locke's Two Treatises of Government* (Cambridge, 1989).

Ashley, Maurice, *The Glorious Revolution of 1688* (London, 1966).

Ashley, Maurice, *James II* (London, 1977).

Baxter, S. B., *The Development of the Treasury: 1660–1702* (London, 1957).

Baxter, S. B., *William III* (London, 1966).

Baxter, S.B., *William III and the Defense of European Liberty, 1650–1702* (New York, 1966).

Beddard, Robert, 'Anti-Popery and the London Mob, 1688', *History Today* (1988), 36–9.

Clifton, R., *The Last Popular Rebellion: The Western Rising of 1685* (London, 1984).

Corish, P. W., *The Catholic Community in the Seventeenth and Eighteenth Centuries* (Dublin, 1981).

Cottret, Bernard, *La Glorieuse Révolution d'Angleterre, 1688* (Paris, 1988).

Cullen, L. M., *The Emergence of Modern Ireland, 1600–1900* (London, 1981).

Dickinson, H. T. 'The Eighteenth Century Debate on the "Glorious Revolution"', *History*, LXI (1976), 28–45.

Dickinson, H. T., 'The Eighteenth-Century Debate on the Sovereignty of Parliament', *TRHS*, 5th ser. (1976), 189–210.

Doebner, R. (ed.), *Memoirs of Mary, Queen of England (1689–1693)* (London, 1886).

Doherty, Richard, *The Williamite War in Ireland, 1689–91* (Dublin, 1998).

Dunn, John, *The Political Thought of John Locke: An Historical Account of the Argument of the Two Treatises on Government* (Cambridge, 1969).

Earle, Peter, *Monmouth's Rebellion* (London, 1977).

Erskine-Hill, Howard, *Poetry and the Realm of Politics: Shakespeare to Dryden* (Oxford, 1996).

Ferguson, W., *Scotland's Relations with England: A Survey to 1707* (Edinburgh, 1977).

Figgis, John Neville, *The Divine Right of Kings* (New York, 1965).

Garrett, Jane, *The Triumphs of Providence: The Assassination Plot of 1696* (Cambridge, 1980).

Goldie, Mark, 'Edmund Bohun and the *Jus Gentium* in the Revolution Debate, 1689–1693', *HJ*, XX (1977), 569–86.

Grell, O., Israel, J. J. and Tyacke, N. (eds), *From Toleration to Persecution. The Glorious Revolution and Religion in England* (Oxford, 1991).

Haley, K. H. D., *The First Earl of Shaftesbury* (Oxford, 1968).

Harris, Tim, *Politics under the Later Stuarts: Party Conflicts in a Divided Society, 1660–1715* (London, 1993).

Holmes, Geoffrey (ed.), *Britain after the Glorious Revolution, 1689–1714* (London, 1969).

Horwitz, Henry, 'Parliament and the Glorious Revolution', *BIHR*, XLVII (1974), 36–52.

Horwitz, Henry, '1689 (and all that)', *Parliamentary History*, VI (1987), 23–32.

Jones, D. W., *War and Economy in the Age of William III and Marlborough* (Oxford, 1988).

Jones, G. H., 'The Irish Fright of 1688', *BIHR*, LV (1982), 148–57.

Jones, J. R., *Country and Court: England 1658–1714* (London, 1978).

Jones, J. R. (ed.), *The Restored Monarchy 1660–1688* (London, 1979).

Jones, J. R., *Charles II: Royal Politician* (London, 1987).

Keeton, G. W., *Lord Chancellor Jeffreys and the Stuart Cause* (London, 1965).

Kishlansky, Mark, *A Monarchy Transformed: Britain 1603–1714* (London, 1997).

Lacey, Douglas R., *Dissent and Parliamentary Politics in England, 1661–1688* (New Brunswick, 1969).

Laslett, Peter (ed.), *John Locke, Two Treatises of Government* (Cambridge, 1991).

LeFevre, P., 'Tangier, the Navy and its Connection with the Glorious Revolution', *Mariner's Mirror*, LXXIII (1987), 187–90.

Lenman, Bruce, *The Jacobite Risings in Britain 1689–1746* (London, 1980).

Linklater, Magnus and Christian, Lady Hesketh, *For King and Conscience: John Graham of Claverhouse, Viscount Dundee* (London, 1989).

Miller, John, *James II: A Study in Kingship* (Hove, 1977).

Miller, John, 'The Glorious Revolution: "Contract" and "Abdication" Reconsidered', *HJ*, XXV (1982), 341–55.

Miller, John, *The Glorious Revolution* (London, 1983).

Miller, John, 'The Potential for "Absolutism" in later Stuart England', *History*, LXIX (1984), 187–207.

Monod, Paul, *Jacobitism and the English People, 1688–1788* (Cambridge, 1989).

Nenner, Howard, *By Colour of Law* (Chicago, 1977).

Nenner, Howard, 'The Traces of Shame in England's Glorious Revolution', *History*, LXXIII (1988), 238–47.

O'Callaghan, John, *History of the Irish Brigades in the Service of France* (Dublin, 1854).

Ogg, David, *England in the Reign of Charles II* (Oxford, 1955–56).

Pocock, J. G. A., *The Ancient Constitution and the Feudal Law: A Study of English Political Thought in the Seventeenth Century* (Cambridge, 1987).

Pocock, J. G. A., 'The Fourth English Civil War: Dissolution, Desertion and Alternative Histories in the Glorious Revolution', *Government and Opposition: A Journal of Comparative Politics*, XXIII (1988), 51–66.

Prebble, J., *The Darien Disaster* (London, 1968).

Riley, P. W. J., *King William and the Scottish Ministers* (Edinburgh, 1979).

Robbins, Caroline, *The Eighteenth Century Commonwealth Man* (Cambridge, MA, 1959).

Roseveare, Henry, *The Financial Revolution, 1660–1760* (London, 1991).

Schwoerer, Lois G., 'Women and the Glorious Revolution', *Albion*, XVIII (1986), 197–218.

Schwoerer, Lois G., 'Locke, Lockean Ideas, and the Glorious Revolution', *Journal of the History of Ideas*, LI (1990), 531–48.

Slaughter, Thomas P., '"Abdicate" and "Contract" in the Glorious Revolution', *HJ*, XXIV (1981), 323–37.

Slaughter, Thomas P., '"Abdicate" and "Contract" Restored', *HJ*, XXVIII (1981), 399–403.

Spurr, John, *The Restoration Church of England, 1660–1689* (New Haven, CT, 1991).

Straka, G. M., *Anglican Reaction to the Revolution of 1688* (State Historical Society, Madison, WI, 1992).

Tarlton, Charles D., '"The Rulers Now on Earth": Locke's *Two Treatises* and the Revolution of 1688', *HJ*, XXVIII (1985), 279–98.

Turner, F. C., *James II* (London, 1948).

Western, J. R., *Monarchy and Revolution: The English State in the 1680s* (London, 1972).

INDEX